THE
BEDSIDE
BOOK OF
DORMERS

and
other delights

THE BEDSIDE BOOK OF DORMERS

and
other delights

A Pictorial Guide to
Traditional Architectural Details in Ulster

Marcus Patton

ULSTER ARCHITECTURAL HERITAGE SOCIETY
Belfast   2011

First published 2011 by the Ulster Architectural Heritage Society,
66 Donegall Pass, Belfast BT7 1BU

EDITOR   Karen Latimer
DESIGN   Grand Piano Press
PRINT   W&G Baird Ltd

This publication was printed using FSC certified paper, sourced from sustainably managed forests.

ISBN
978-0-900457-74-6 (Hard)
978-0-900457-75-3 (Soft)

A CIP catalogue record for this book is available from the British Library.

Frontispiece: Market Square, Dungannon

Water colour by Marcus Patton, 1979

Dungannon Police Station (on the right) was reputedly designed for use in the Khyber Pass in India, but the plans got misplaced due to a clerical error by a civil servant in Dublin. Local legend has it that the Khyber Pass is decorated by an Ulster police station.

MARC FITCH FUND

THE ESMÉ MITCHELL TRUST

NIEA
Northern Ireland
Environment
Agency
www.doeni.gov.uk/niea

An Agency within the Department of the
Environment
www.doeni.gov.uk

Contents

Foreword

This book that Marcus Patton has assembled illustrates and records a selection from the mass of details that enliven the built environment of our cities, towns, villages and countryside. Some of the details are architect-led and inspired, a few are mass produced and were sold from catalogues (these volumes are often works of beauty in their own right), but most are the work of local craftsmen, indeed in some instances they could be given the accolade not of craftsman but of artist.

Most of the examples illustrated date from the 19th century and the first quarter of the 20th. A few fall off one or other end of that scale. It is difficult to generalise about their origins and development or even the driving force behind their creation but they do tend to relate to a period when landlords were in an "improving" mode. Lodges, estate workers cottages, follies and many other similar constructions were going up all over the country and no doubt this encouraged the inventiveness and imagination of local craftsmen. The Gothick Revival, as well as the Romantic and Picturesque were all the rage and these styles left a good deal of scope for inventiveness within the basic form and framework, in much the same way that folk tales may share a common root yet are adapted in the telling for the benefit of a specific audience.

In the second half of the 19th century, the captains of industry began to take up the baton. The railways companies, for example, encouraged local creativity. There were many manifestations - think of the coach builders and sign writers. I realise that I am straying beyond the bounds of the present study but the strong individual character of many of our graveyards, created by the work of local monumental masons, has often struck me. No doubt there is material here for a volume two if not a three or four.

Many of the tools used by these creative men are themselves works of art. Indeed it was a requirement of many apprenticeships that the young man made his own tools as part of his education, and they often became a labour of love. Over the years, I have developed a particular interest in wrought ironwork and so I am especially pleased to see this industry well represented in these pages. Of all the regions of the British Isles, Ireland has the strongest tradition in this field.

Too often we trudge our streets and roadways staring at our boots. If nothing else, Marcus, in this book, is encouraging us to look up to enjoy the feast of pleasures above. Better still, it should lead us to cherish and care for these flights of fancy and when the spirit moves us, even to add to this great tradition in our own individual ways.

Richard Oram

**The fragility of traditional buildings -
Trillick, Co Fermanagh, 2001**

The digger approached the building like a dinosaur crouching close to its prey, then it took a snoop (as the Marx Bros would call it) out of one side, then another, and then a bite at rafters and slates, and at the chimney, then some front wall, and in barely ten minutes the digger was sitting on top of the ruins in a pile of dust, like an animal in on the kill. It was pretty shocking, knowing that restoring a building like that (in not such good condition), or even building a replacement bungalow behind it, would take six months.

Preface
& Acknowledgements

When I came back to Northern Ireland in 1978 after some years of living in Scotland I was pleased to recognise architectural details that I had missed elsewhere, and often delighted by other things I had never noticed before. I was in a wonderful new job that required me to travel across Northern Ireland looking at historic buildings at risk, and before long I was photographing details of plenty of other buildings too as I came across them.

I could not have defined exactly what I was recording, because many of them were not listed buildings, and often the details were not "correct". The buildings themselves were often rundown or even derelict, and indeed I often found the most interesting building in a town was also the most neglected. Of course, it was interesting precisely because it was neglected - no one had removed or tidied up the features that gave it the character of a particular period or personality.

Our more spectacular buildings have long been recognised as important, but sometimes it takes an outsider to appreciate the quieter and more common ones. An Australian cousin who was an avid bird-twitcher recently visited us for his first trip to the UK, and having seen the exotic and brightly-coloured birds he was used to at home we expected him to find our small and dun-coloured birdlife somewhat tedious. Of course he found it nothing of the kind - the birds were all new to him, and he was intrigued to learn about their habits and relationships. This book is (for the most part) about those hedge sparrows that we take for granted but which visitors to Ireland can find surprisingly exotic.

Part of the fascination of putting this book together has been the process of defining these elements and trying to work out a sort of Linnaean system for them. Of course it is not a very scientific exercise, as human taste and ambition rather than evolutionary success have dictated the sequence of events, but the process of defining and naming the variations helps to make them more visible. Before we married

9

my wife had not noticed bargeboards because she didn't know what they were called, and one of the more esoteric excitements of our honeymoon in Fermanagh was spotting new varieties of bargeboard displaying their brightly coloured plumages in the soft rain.

It should be emphasised that this is not a design guide - some of the details included in the book do not work very well, and others are plug-ugly. Nor are they all local vernaculars - many of the details derive from Classical or Gothic originals built elsewhere, and they are not all unique to Ulster. Some of them are not even particularly old, although most pre-date that great chronological divide, the First World War. However taken as a whole they do have a flavour that you can recognise as Ulster, as distinctive as potato farls, and our towns and villages would be the poorer without their cheerful presence.

It may not be a design guide, but I hope there are still lessons to be learned from the book. Readers will recognise building materials that are used in one part of Ulster or another, and perhaps styles and a sort of vocabulary that is local to their county. Where a building is missing a detail, the reader may locate a template here that is of similar date and style, or there may be inspiration to create a new detail that draws upon these models. There is no substitute for looking at the originals of course, to establish just how deep or chunky or surprisingly big a detail actually is - a photograph tends to flatten out the third dimension that makes the difference between an accurate reproduction and a poor pastiche.

This is more like a dictionary of slang, making no value judgements (well, hardly any) on crude excrescences and visual malapropisms, but relishing the vitality of the language and the people that produced it. Purists may shudder, but I hope the book throws a spotlight on our surviving traditional details and encourages their preservation. Unlike a dictionary, however, it is not a comprehensive catalogue as it relies on photographs that for the most part were taken opportunistically, when I happened to visit a new village and often in poor weather. Furthermore, rather than defining typical details, the examples tend to concentrate on the variants and oddities that add spice to the ordinary, and so are statistically quite unrepresentative.

It could be used like a pocket I-Spy book, because few of the buildings are identified, and only located by (nearest) town and county. Details can be hard to recognise taken out of context, and to make the game more difficult it has to be said that many of these buildings no longer exist. I took thousands of these photographs in the early 1980s and it would have been impossible to take better photographs of many of them today because even if the buildings have not been demolished the details have been shaved off so many of them. Please bear with the poor quality of some of those photographs as in some cases they are the only record of details that have been lost.

For the most permanent of the arts, architecture is remarkably transient. The basic structure of a building may survive a long time but brick gets repointed, glass gets broken, slates slip, timber rots and even stone decays. And that is only if a building doesn't go out of fashion and become altered or demolished long before it has reached its physical sell-by date. Part of the fascination of old buildings is tracing the ways in which they have been altered - sometimes for the better, often for the worse. What makes these details special is that having once been quite typical they are now rare. So many of our indigenous window types for instance have been wiped out by plastic windows, the grey squirrel of the architectural ecosystem, and our buildings are less individual and interesting as a result. When fashions change and we get down to our last plastic window I'll be out there photographing it. But not till then.

This book has been a long time in the gestation, and I am grateful to many people who have helped to analyse or date examples in the course of discussions and lectures. In particular, thanks are due to Charlie Brett and the committee of Hearth who brought me back from Scotland and provided me with the stimulus to look afresh at our architectural heritage. Charlie knew more about Ulster architecture than most Ulster architects do, and I learnt a great deal from him about the history and aesthetics of our buildings - not to mention the fun to be had from exploring them. My thanks are also due to Michael Longley and the Arts Council of Northern Ireland, who provided a grant for my early researches into the subject, and to David Evans who helped to define the subject when we were working on a previous book for the UAHS, *The Diamond as Big as a Square*. Andrew McClelland and Rita Harkin helped with my first attempts to make sense of the pile of material, and we spent some pleasant afternoons classifying dormers as submarines or kangaroos, and bargeboards as wavy, frilly or fretted. When it looked as if it might become a book Dick Oram provided encouragement and wise comments; his enthusiasm for building construction was intense and his knowledge deep. He looked over early drafts shortly before his untimely death, and had taken some photographs of details himself that I have been able to include in the volume. And as ever I owe a debt of gratitude to Karen Latimer, who has edited the book with her usual speed, tact, efficiency and encouragement.

The Society is indebted to the funders of this book - The Esmé Mitchell Trust, the Marc Fitch Fund and the Northern Ireland Environment Agency - who have made it possible to produce this highly illustrated book. We gratefully acknowledge legacies from Sir Charles Brett and Mr John Greer. Legacies provide financial stability to the UAHS and allow it to continue its vital role of promoting the appreciation and retention of the best of our built heritage.

Finally I have David Evans to thank again for the title of the book, which he came up with long before the book itself had taken shape. It is of course about much more than dormers, and I hope it will be lifted with a degree of pleasure from coffee tables and bookshelves as well as bedsides.

MP

Windows

Windows are, famously, the eyes of a house. The arrangement and proportions of windows and their design are the single most important factor in determining the feeling of a building, and will often give important clues about its age and cultural influences.

Although the double-hung sash window is the most common type to be found in historic buildings in Ulster, earlier types such as fixed lights or casement windows are also sometimes found, and in rural houses the sashes are often not counterbalanced but have to be propped open. The variety of fenestration from small panes to plate glass is enormous, and the materials range from timber to cast iron or even steel.

The increased use of standardised plastic windows has led to the loss of many historic windows that had been in use for a hundred years or more and only needed repair. The new windows are often crude in the thickness of their glazing bars and frames, and they lack the depth of older windows where the lower sashes are set behind the upper ones or within deep reveals. Above all, they lack the sheer variety of the designs that follow.

Hillsborough, Co Down

This terrace of houses demonstrates typical Georgian proportions with small top floor windows, the main living room room on the first floor, the panelled door with fanlight and a basement kitchen and scullery. The windows are all small-paned double-hung sashes.

Ballywalter, Co Down

In a vernacular cottage like this windows are small, punched through only where necessary, and vary in size and proportion. The slate roof, probably originally thatched, is tarred over.

Bangor, Co Down

Early town houses which appear to be single-storey but in fact, as the high wallhead indicates, there are first floor bedrooms lit by skylights.

Ballycastle, Co Antrim

A typical three-storey Georgian building with its main windows on the first floor and smaller second floor ones.

Dundrum, Co Down

Sometimes the first floor windows are emphasised as here with more elaborate surrounds and larger panes added.

Comber, Co Down

In this late 18th century terrace windows and doors are squashed with considerable *joie de vivre* into the available space.

Rostrevor, Co Down

In vernacular cottages, the half door also served as a window, letting in light and air when many windows were fixed.

Teemore, Co Fermanagh

In mud-built cottages like this, window openings had to be small and often could not be opened.

Lehinch, Co Fermanagh

Although this window is also fixed, its semi-circular form is more sophisticated and playful.

Portavogie, Co Down

This cottage has a variety of windows from fixed ones like this to conventional sash windows, all set deep in the walls.

Comber, Co Down

Although quite a sophisticated piece of joinery this ground floor window is a fixed light.

Glenanne, Co Armagh

Early 19th century outbuildings and mills often had cast-iron windows, sometimes quite ornamental.

Comber, Co Down

The window above a door, known as the fanlight, was a source of light to the hall.

Caledon, Co Tyrone

Diamond lattices in casement windows were common in estate buildings, giving a romantic olde-worlde effect.

Castleward, Co Down

Dating from 1832, this window has a neo-Elizabethan label over casements with playful fleur-de-lis.

Lisnaskea, Co Fermanagh

In the latter part of the 19th century casements were often combined with stone mullions to create the appearance of a Jacobean manor. Here the elegant design of the casements is echoed in the fanlight over the door.

Cookstown, Co Tyrone

By Edwardian times the mullions only need to be timber as steel was available to span the large opening.

Antrim, Co Antrim

The first sliding sash windows were probably horizontal ones like this at the back of an 18th century house. The invention of counterbalance weights made vertical sashes possible.

Antrim, Co Antrim

Early double-hung (ie, both sashes counterbalanced) windows had exposed sash-boxes that were later set behind the reveals. This example is later than the one on the right.

Comber, Co Down

This double-hung window is of an early date, with the sash-boxes set flush with the face of the wall, and no horns on the sashes. Note the timber lintel too.

Bleary, Co Down

The standard small-pane sash window has this "six over six" arrangement of panes, but there are many alternatives.

Cushendall, Co Antrim

A layout with eight-pane sashes suits wide windows, or as here may simply reflect the cost of large panes.

Rostrevor, Co Down

This unusual fenestration with four-pane sashes suggests a date shortly before the arrival of plate glass.

Bessbrook, Co Armagh

The reduced height of upper floor windows often suits this pattern of "three over six" above conventional ground floor windows. Pairs of "wally dugs" normally frequent the mantelpiece but are here enjoying the view.

Derrykerrib, Co Fermanagh

In this "three over three" window the greater width of the central pane is a precursor of the Victorian margin pane.

Newcastle, Co Down

A margin-paned fixed light, with the more expensive central panes placed to get the best view.

Warrenpoint, Co Down

An extreme version of margin pane, suggesting that the arrangement is decorative rather than economical.

Cookstown, Co Tyrone

Exuberant railway station architecture from 1879, with the upper margin echoing the segmental head of the opening.

College Gardens, Belfast

Elegant late Victorian margin panes set in blocked architrave surrounds, giving the windows extra definition.

Sion Mills, Co Tyrone

Ballycastle, Co Antrim

Once sheet glass was available plain sashes became the norm and many older sashes were upgraded. With the glass in a single pane, attention turns to the window setting, enhanced in the example on the right with a chamfered lintel.

Glenarm, Co Antrim

Most earlier styles of architecture were revived in the 19th century. This mock-mediaeval barbican has lancet windows.

Old Holywood Road, Belfast

Bellarena, Co L'derry

These lancet windows are on a larger scale, but the narrow proportions and vertical emphasis suit the Victorian aesthetic. In the Bellarena example the verticality is further emphasied by the margin panes.

Markethill, Co Armagh

The Norman style was rarely used here in Victorian times, the best example being the neo-Norman Gosford Castle.

Donegall Street, Belfast

The Gothic Revival focused on ecclesiastical and education buildings, such as this one with its massive timber traceries and mullioned windows set below the central gable and clock.

Ballyveridagh, Co Antrim

Now located in the Ulster Folk & Transport Museum, this Gothick school-house originally stood near Ballycastle.

Antrim, Co Antrim

Larger Gothick windows in a church (with traces of its name in the shield above), here converted to a warehouse.

Rostrevor, Co Down

A romantic Gothic Revival window in a domestic setting, complete with eyebrow label and heads on bosses.

Dungannon, Co Tyrone

Following the example of Sir Walter Scott at Abbotsford private houses could enjoy string courses and helmeted heads.

Great Victoria Street, Belfast

May Street, Belfast

The influence of John Ruskin's enthusiasm for Venetian Gothic was noticeable in 1860s Belfast with these examples of banded brick and stonework and the plate tracery of the Diocesan Offices on the right.

Royal Avenue, Belfast

All the tricks of the terracotta repertoire are brought out in this tour de force of barley-sugar columns and cinquefoils.

Tudor Place, Belfast

An appropriately depressed arch for this neo-Tudor window, set inside a conventional rectangular opening.

Hilden, Co Antrim

Tudor here turns Moorish with an ogee-arched opening, and delicate matching bargeboard and finial.

Stewartstown, Co Tyrone

By 1900 large sheets of glass were available, but it was fashionable to put small panes in the upper sash.

Comber, Co Down

Paired Arts & Crafts windows set in an arched opening, with a corbel setting off the broad central mullion.

Coleraine, Co L'derry

In the 1930s it was common to mix brick with rendered walls, as in this window.

Antrim, Co Antrim

In this simple house, probably dating from the end of the 19th century, the double-hung sash windows have a segmental-arched timber head set in the usual rectangular opening, adding a touch of elegance very simply.

Lurgan, Co Armagh

This picture shows how a conventional rectangular window can be set behind an arched opening.

Ballynahinch, Co Down

A sash window recessed behind its reveals and neatly set off with a slender moulding emphasising the arch.

Ballynahinch, Co Down

A bit more than a window but a bit less than a surround, this incorporates slender columns and an entablature.

Comber, Co Down

The window is segmental-arched, but the moulding round it softens to the shape of a basket-handle.

Moneymore, Co L'derry

A simple window, almost round-headed and divided vertically, is set off by the more elaborate grained Victorian doorcase with its corbels and blocked panels, set within another round-headed arch.

Limavady, Co L'derry

A busy shopper resists the temptation of these ornamental basket-headed windows.

Saintfield, Co Down

A simple round-headed window in a busy main street creates an intriguing display.

Downpatrick, Co Down

This early (1735) round-headed window with its Gibbsian blocking-pieces over the arch, still has Gothic fenestration.

Armagh, Co Armagh

Slightly later (1770), this round-headed window set in a severely Classical building has spokes like a fanlight.

Lurgan, Co Armagh

By 1860 the head of a round-arched window would often contain a roundel rather than spokes.

Victoria Street, Belfast

Although built as a mere seed warehouse, this building is lavishly covered in sculpture, set off by the ornamental ironwork in the round-headed window openings. It is set in front of the actual windows and incorporates the owner's monogram.

Newcastle, Co Down

A broad window delicately subdivided by the colonette and roundel with sculpted spandrels.

Ballycastle, Co Antrim

Royal Avenue, Belfast

A compromise between the aesthetic need for round-headed arches and the functional requirement for rectangular windows neatly met here, with the opportunity taken to decorate the resulting space.

Portallo Street, Belfast
Horizontally-divided windows are usually modified six-pane sashes and traces of the glazing bars may be visible.

Portaferry, Co Down
Picking out the frame of a window in a contrasting colour is an effective way of brightening up a building.

Mullylusty, Co Fermanagh
Small windows like this would never have had six-pane sashes, and simple vertical divisions are common. Years of painting and repairs have blurred the crispness of the glazing bars, but the layers of limewash on the walls are beautiful.

Newtownards, Co Down

If you have enough books you don't miss seeing out of the window, and they make excellent insulation.

Mullan, Co Monaghan

Some say that bottles have a similar effect, particularly when full.

Dungannon, Co Tyrone

A wide curved window in a shallow bow. Probably early 19th century, the curve is provided by timber rather than glass.

Cornmarket, Belfast

Waring Street, Belfast

From around 1860 plate glass became available and soon sophisticated curved glass was possible, the window on the right dating from about 1870. As well as enabling interesting corners, curved glass catches the light brilliantly.

East Bridge Street, Belfast

A round-headed window in a curved wall provided a few challenges for its builders.

Ballynahinch, Co Down

Iron lent itself readily to ornamental fixed lights, often used in churches and schools.

Charlemont, Co Armagh

The ready availability of cast iron from the end of the 18th century made possible elegant but mass-produced windows like this. Set above stone cills and glazed with crown glass they are delightful and durable.

Killyman, Co Tyrone

When an opening light was required iron sashes could be hung as casements, usually in timber sub-frames.

Charlemont, Co Armagh

Although having the appearance of conventional sash windows, the weight of iron usually dictated pivot hinges.

Mowhan, Co Armagh

Here the wooden sub-frame and metal sashes can be clearly seen, with the pivot arrangement of the upper sash.

Castlederg, Co Tyrone

A similar window seen from the inside, with the thumb-turn in the mid-rail to secure the upper sash.

Castlederg, Co Tyrone

A twenty-pane iron pivot window in a one-time factory later converted to housing.

Finaghy, Co Antrim

More suitable for domestic use were leaded lights, often set in stone mullions as here.

Kircubbin, Co Down

Steel windows were introduced in the 1930s and were light and strong. Unfortunately they also tend to rust, and many were replaced in different materials.

Bangor, Co Down

Fashionable elements from the 1920s include the porthole, the hard-edged windows and the stylish porch.

Bangor, Co Down

The sleek corner remains, but the streamlined windows have lost their 1930s horizontal steel bands.

Bangor, Co Down

The full height staircase window with the asymmetric blank wall beside it speak of the post-war era.

Stranmillis Road, Belfast

A timber opening porthole window with its protective eyelid frame above - quite a common feature of Deco buildings.

Ballynahinch, Co Down

A Victorian porthole, set under the eaves and elongated into an oval.

University Road, Belfast

A staircase expressed functionally, Victorian-style - you can almost count the steps in the brickwork.

Ormeau Road, Belfast

A blank quatrefoil decorates a wall in a position where there is no need for an actual window.

Saintfield, Co Down

A trefoil window picked out in red sandstone. The date is in the 1890s, but it could have been a lot older.

Holywood, Co Down

One of the problems of houses masquerading as Classical buildings is the difficulty of lighting attics discreetly.

Bangor, Co Down

Bangor, Co Down

The Arts & Crafts styled building on the left has unusual first-floor windows that could almost be Diocletian (a semicircular window type developed by the Romans) - fully realised in the modernistic building on the right that dates from the 1920s. Note the porthole and exaggerated keystones at first floor.

Newtownards, Co Down

A true Palladian window built in 1765 - as used by the Renaissance architect Andrea Palladio.

Enniskillen, Co Fermanagh

An interpretation of Palladian executed in timber (with a modernistic flash of bricks under the eaves).

Armagh, Co Armagh; Dyan, Co Tyrone; and Hillsborough, Co Down

Variations on Palladian windows with the theme of the tall central light - as seen in a brick-built shop, an Orange Hall and a private house with a very surprised-looking expression.

Armagh, Co Armagh

A terrace of early 18th century houses at Armagh Cathedral appears to have conventional fixed windows under the eaves, but (right) the sash lifts vertically into the body of the wall. As there is no counterbalance the window is wedged open.

Cushendall, Co Antrim

A unique arrangement where the window projects from the wall, permitting trap-doors at its base to see the street below.

Bellaghy, Co L'derry

Painted windows rather than exposed blockwork or timber while a building awaits new uses.

Donaghmore, Co Down

A fully glazed blind window with dark timber behind it retains the symmetry of the building without losing wall space.

Annalong, Co Down

A tin-clad house, the mundane materials painted in magnificently bright colours that still fit into the countryside.

Antrim, Co Antrim **Antrim, Co Antrim** **Comber, Co Down**

Moving on from the actual window to its setting, the simplest treatment is to chamfer the reveals, creating interesting shadows around the opening. In brickwork (*left*) this requires the use of special bricks, but it is easily carried out in plaster, whether with margin panes (*centre*) or Arts & Crafts sashes.

Belcoo, Co Fermanagh **Downpatrick, Co Down** **Draperstown, Co L'derry**

The central stone of an arch is called the keystone, and in a flat arch it is particularly important in keeping the arch together. The keystones above are of course entirely false, and one (*left*) is merely painted. The *central* one is a facet on the architrave that catches the light, and that on the *right* is unusual in being set on its own entablature.

Warrenpoint, Co Down

At first sight a conventional keystone - but the decoration looks like the medical caduceus - did the doctor live here?

Newtownabbey, Co Antrim

The use of vine leaves and grapes suggests good hospitality, and they are often found in dining rooms.

Holywood, Co Down

This keystone is more like a crest on top of the window architrave, perhaps suggesting a rising sun.

Newry, Co Down

A scallop shell applied to the architrave, adding a sculptural element to the window surround.

Lurgan, Co Armagh

These solicitors occupy a vivacious polychrome brick building, the keystones of which are Eastern potentates.

Cookstown, Co Tyrone

A strange gargoyle-like creature crouches on the architrave - but see much more of this later (*see* p.315).

Fivemiletown, Co Tyrone

The square eyebrow motif seen here (often known as a label) was a standard feature of Tudor buildings.

Strangford, Co Down

The label motif is seen here in flat brickwork, no longer throwing rainwater off the window as intended.

Castlerock, Co L'derry

Set under a deep eaves this label has a Gothic arch to suit its window.

Lurgan, Co Armagh

Although labels normally have splayed ends, this one has vertical sides terminating in bosses.

Glenallen Street, Belfast

Taking advantage of the ease of moulding plaster, this eyebrow has additional ornament over the window.

Stranmillis Road, Belfast

This is a sort of minimalist eyebrow, shallow and without angles, but ornamented by stripes (and a pigeon).

Comber, Co Down

A flat arch over an opening like this is called a soldier arch (though traditionally the soldiers topple over at each end).

Carmel Street, Belfast

More commonly the arch is slightly raised like this, and the combination of arch and supports highly varied.

Ballynahinch, Co Down

Here bands of red and cream brick alternate rather like quoinstones, contrasting with the surrounding stone.

Botanic Avenue, Belfast

In polychrome (coloured brick) buildings there are so many decorative options that the window can be quite plain.

Ardenvohr Street, Belfast

Normally two windows side by side will be linked with decorative brick or mouldings, but here, whether from a scarcity of yellow bricks or indecision about the best way forward, there is a hiatus. The reveals aren't even symmetrical.

Armagh, Co Armagh

A formal window opening in a random rubble wall - with long and short quoins and a flat arch of voussoir stones.

Bangor, Co Down

Though rendered, this building is of rubble stone, and the simple window surrounds are cut stone.

Coalisland, Co Tyrone

In rendered buildings all sorts of fanciful surrounds are possible, often picked out in colours contrasting with the walls.

Castlewellan, Co Down

A particularly neat and sophisticated mock surround that only exists in paintwork.

Glenarm, Co Antrim

A fluted plaster surround with shrugging shoulders and kicked-out base, contrasting with rougher render.

Bangor, Co Down

A sentry-box architrave with circles at the shoulders and whorls at the base, part of some fine rendering.

Woodstock Road, Belfast

Sombre vermiculated quoins and keystone in plaster, matched by swirling stained glass in the window.

Oxford Street, Belfast

Rather Mannerist decoration, with round-headed windows on a corner and surrounds that don't reach the base.

Newtownards, Co Down

A surround incorporating lavish vegetable decoration, made still more noticeable with this paint scheme.

Florenceville Avenue, Belfast

A formal surround with projecting lintel ends and corbels under the cills, decorated with plants at the roundels.

Derry, Co L'derry

An unusual moulded surround with a deep base and smooth curves making it look like a spaceship.

Donegall Square South, Belfast

The centrepiece of this richly decorated warehouse of about 1865 is a nymph sitting between the paired windows.

39

Ballygawley, Co Tyrone

A light-hearted window surround decorated with mussel-shells, contrasting with the hard-edged chrome lettering.

Newtownbutler, Co Fermanagh

A façade can be unified by setting a variety of doors and windows within similar arched recesses.

Ballykelly, Co L'derry

Sometimes windows are set in recesses that were formerly doors, but this appears to be an original detail.

Bangor, Co Down

On the left, a conventional reeded architrave with superimposed blocks; on the right the same detail recessed behind the face of the central bay, producing a strangely frivolous effect for a former courthouse.

Downpatrick, Co Down

This unusual detail is a sort of negative keystone, almost as if it is supporting a wall that isn't there.

Coleraine, Co L'derry

The basic surround can be decorated by corbels below the cill and crests, usually of plants, over the head.

Antrim, Co Antrim

This almost Baroque surround is topped by a selection of cut flowers stuck into the entablature.

Newry, Co Down

A tall surround with scrolled bases and a segmental-headed entablature supported on corbels.

Lurgan, Co Armagh

Two windows with very different decoration - a simple surround with scrolled base above, heavy entablature below.

Donegall Square South, Belfast

A flat entablature decorated with a rich swag of vegetation. Note a further elaborate frieze under the eaves.

College Green, Belfast

A grand tripartite window with scrolls and a porthole (here perhaps more of an oeil de boeuf) over the entablature.

Cromac Square, Belfast

When the top of the surround is thrown forward like this it is known as an entablature.

Cromac Square, Belfast

The entablature is often supported on corbels at the sides, with an ornamental panel placed between them.

Lurgan, Co Armagh

Sometimes the corbels are almost more important than the entablature, and sometimes there are no pilasters.

Newtownards, Co Down

A fully equipped window with entablature, corbels, surround, and keystone and window-guard joining in.

Camden Street, Belfast

Although a typical corbel is an S-shaped scroll, sometimes fluted and sometimes not, the range of corbels is wide. The examples above are abstract, but vegetable or leafy decoration is quite common.

Dungannon, Co Tyrone

In this example the corbels are almost as big as the pilasters that support them, but that creates a confident swagger.

Armagh, Co Armagh

Here the corbels support pediments (closed on the *left*, open on the *right*). Banks like these are particularly fond of pediments, often alternating triangular and semicircular pediments in the approved Classical style.

Ballynahinch, Co Down

Bangor, Co Down

Occasionally the top of an entablature is extended and decorated with mock-slates. The resulting confection is called an aedicule, or little house. On this stuccowork the pediment protects a date and scrolls enclose other windows.

Bangor, Co Down

Simple aedicules over first-floor windows - the smaller upper floor ones only merit shouldered architraves.

Comber, Co Down

Randalstown, Co Antrim

Moira, Co Down

When two windows occur side by side (*left*) there are numerous ways to combine them: sharing a common pilaster (*centre*) or a common label moulding (*right*). Either way they let in plenty of light and share the view without creating the blank façade presented by the modern picture window.

Coleraine, Co L'derry

In this building of 1869 the windows are divided by a slender colonette supporting simple lintels.

Great Victoria Street, Belfast

This column has more work to do with the deep banded semi-circular heads of the window.

Kircubbin, Co Down

The colonette in this case is probably not structural as the lintel will span both windows.

Comber, Co Down (*above*)

Derry, Co L'derry (*left*)

High Victorian and Arts & Crafts respectively, with central colonettes.

Ormeau Road, Belfast

Even more varied patterns are possible when three windows coincide, as in this vaguely Romanesque grouping.

Tandragee, Co Armagh   **Markethill, Co Armagh**

Ballywalter, Co Down

A common arrangement is the tripartite window, where the broad central sashes are usually counterbalanced and the narrow sidelights not. That arrangement keeps the mullions light as only one set of pulleys has to be housed in them.

In grander Victorian houses the tripartite window could be disguised as a Classical portico.

Kircubbin, Co Down

The broader mullions here suggest that the sidelights are fully counterbalanced, but the surround keeps the design light.

Rosetta Park, Belfast

Seen from the inside, this tripartite window has a large semicircle of leaded glass above it.

Cookstown, Co Tyrone

A remarkable exposition on the tripartite window, with three solutions to the problem of arches of different widths.

Seaforde, Co Down

Curiously, the central light of this window was blind, being occupied by the party wall between two houses.

Killyleagh, Co Down

This later window has toplights and casements, leaving the mullions light, but the eye is distracted by the surround.

Ballywalter, Co Down

Three windows are often the beginning of an arcade, such as on Lynn's bank of 1855 (*top right*) with its mediaeval heads, or the extraordinary abstract decoration in Castle Place, almost Art Deco in feeling but dating from about 1870.

Warrenpoint, Co Down (*above*)
Newtownards, Co Down (*top right*)
Lisburn Road, Belfast (*centre right*)
Castle Place, Belfast (*bottom right*)

as

Downpatrick, Co Down

Bow windows appeared in the 18th century, providing good views and drawing light from more angles.

Coleraine, Co L'derry

Early bow fronts were shallow, and usually for shops to display their wares better.

Bangor, Co Down

As the 19th century went on, bow windows became more rounded in plan. (This example is from 1865).

Ardglass, Co Down

Canted bay windows were easier to construct than bows and soon became more common. This charming example is unusually constructed of wood.

Bangor, Co Down

Square bays also became common around 1900, sometimes roofed with slate as here, other times with lead and sometimes parapet roofs.

Palmer Street, Belfast

The little square bay provides extra space to the parlour house, as well as enlivening the townscape.

Bangor, Co Down

Rendered terrace houses with roofed bay windows, each painted slightly different colours.

Bangor, Co Down

Three storey terraces with bay windows running through the ground and first floors were common by 1900.

Lurgan, Co Armagh

Mock fortifications on the top of a domestic bay window - there is probably a lead flat roof behind them.

Newcastle, Co Down

A remarkable seafront bay window terminating in a fishscaled semi-dome against a gable.

Coleraine, Co L'derry

This shallow bow window probably dating from about 1930, echoes the early bows in its modesty.

Bangor, Co Down

Part of a terrace with timber oriel windows supported on brackets, giving views of the sea.

Dundrum, Co Down

An unusual rendered and presumably masonry-built oriel, complete with slate roof and finial.

Strabane, Co Tyrone

Oriels are bay windows that don't reach the ground. The proprietor of this shop could enjoy the views from his oriel when not working.

Coleraine, Co L'derry

A simple wooden oriel window with interestingly a combination of sash windows at the sides and casement windows in the middle. Like many oriels this was set over a shop and illuminated the owner's first floor living room.

Waring Street, Belfast

This ambitious two-storey oriel is a rare example of Norman Shaw style architecture in Belfast.

Bangor, Co Down

A pair of oriels with casement windows opening out to the sea air, and small-pane upper lights.

Enniskillen, Co Fermanagh

Half verandah, half balcony, this oriel seems intended for sitting in rather than looking out through.

Bangor, Co Down

A shallow oriel probably dating from about 1920 and lighting a staircase, with leaded lights for privacy.

Bangor, Co Down

With deep eaves, tiled roof and casement lights, this is part of a self-consciously "Stockbroker's Tudor" house.

Dungannon, Co Tyrone

This shallow oriel is quite modernistic, with its clean lines, scooped base and steel windows.

Belcoo, Co Fermanagh

Most traditional cills are plain and flat (see *below centre*), but sophisticated ones were made with "stooled" ends.

Coleraine, Co L'derry

This window has no surround or entablature but simple corbels under the cill give it style.

Glenanne, Co Armagh

Another plain window in a simple building, made distinctive by ornamenting the cill.

Randalstown, Co Antrim

Donaghadee, Co Down

One of the problems of having a nice window cill is that people sit on it. The answer is to install a window-guard, which may be as simple as the one on the right, or richly ornamented - *see* p.252.

University Street, Belfast

If you fear that your most intimate possessions may be burgled you may also choose to install window bars.

Lisburn Road, Belfast

Many buildings of stone or brick have single stones as lintels over openings; here the lintel has been chamfered.

Glenoe, Co Antrim

In vernacular buildings the lintels are often of timber. Here, unusually, they were of slates set in mortar.

Downpatrick, Co Down

When summers were hot people feared that sun would spoil their furnishings, so external blinds were fitted.

Enniskillen, Co Fermanagh

The screens behind which blinds were set could be ornamental in themselves, as in this example.

Donaghadee, Co Down

The remains of a window, thought to be from the late 17th century, showing the thick glazing bars made at that time.

Broughshane, Co Antrim

The typical 19th century glazing bar is very slender. This moulding is called lamb's tongue.

Ballylane, Co Armagh   **Portavogie, Co Down**   **Gracehill, Co Antrim**

Horns are the projection of the window frame below an upper sash and above a lower sash. Most Georgian windows did not have horns, which the Victorians used to strengthen the window joints and reduce "coggling" when opening shallow windows. Different carpenters had their own methods of forming horns from simple splays to curvaceous projections.

Mullen, Co Monaghan

Very unusual horns with a stacked effect looking almost like spandrels at the corners of the sashes.

Tennant Street, Belfast

External shutters are rare in Ulster, and usually only employed as here for decorative effect. This unusual terrace was built in 1907 with tile-hung gables and casement windows, as well as the picturesquely pierced shutters.

Richhill, Co Armagh

A late 17th century house with very deep reveals in the stone walls.

Portaferry, Co Down

Markethill, Co Armagh

Folding shutters are housed behind the window architraves and form decorative reveals when closed. They are usually secured open with iron bars that keep the panels flat. This example is for a tall window and the shutter is split horizontally.

Elmwood Avenue, Belfast

Occasionally mid-Victorian houses had internal shutters that rose through runners to cover the window.

Glenarm, Co Antrim

A rural cottage with no shutters, but simple varnished boards on the window reveals.

Markethill, Co Armagh

A low first floor window with folding shutters inside a round-headed window.

Royal Avenue, Belfast

One of the problems of windows at high levels is cleaning them, but there are systems to avoid situations like the above, such as the Scottish Simplex mechanism.

Comber, Co Down

A common complaint about old windows is draughts from poor fitting. Secondary glazing as applied above is barely visible outside (*left*) and inside (*right*).

Glenarm, Co Antrim

Another modern-day requirement is for escape windows from certain rooms. The solution in this case was to build a small sash window inside a casement which opens out (*right*) to the correct size, while looking like an ordinary sash window from the outside (*left*).

Derry, Co L'derry **Saintfield, Co Down** **Moy, Co Tyrone**

The classic form of old glass is crown glass, the manufacture of which involved spinning molten glass at the end of a punty or stick. When the glass had cooled it was broken off and the bull's eye (*left*) was the point of connection. That portion of glass was only used in unimportant locations and the thinner glass from the edge was used elsewhere (*centre* and *right*).

Sans Souci Park, Belfast **Queens Road, Belfast**

From about 1830 sheet glass began to replace crown glass, and its distortions and "seeds" or air bubbles (*left*) are still familiar in panes of glass today. From about 1860, plate glass permitted much larger sheets (*right*) as seen in this house of 1900.

A common sight on Belfast windows during the Troubles was a mesh of sellotape to reduce bomb injuries.

Ballyculter, Co Down

Traditional High Victorian stained glass of about 1860, set in a Gothic window. The clear lights ensured brightness.

Derry, Co L'derry

Despite the Victorians' reputation for sombre colours, even churches often had luminous glass in startling combinations.

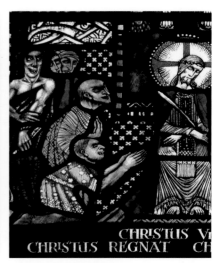

Antrim Road, Belfast

The remarkable Harry Clarke studios produced these idiosyncratic windows in the 1930s.

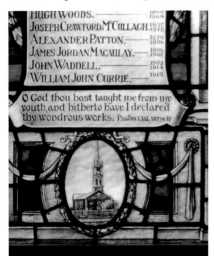

Bangor, Co Down

Church windows occasionally incorporate images of local buildings painted on the glass.

Ballycastle, Co Antrim

Stained glass artists can produce memorable coloured panels in otherwise clear windows.

Ballynahinch, Co Down

The beautiful clear but distorting glass in the quarries (diamond panes) is known as cathedral glass.

Corporation Square, Belfast

Most "stained" glass is actually coloured glass, but the yellow seen so often is a true stain painted on the glass.

Craigavad, Co Down

The effect of white patterns on coloured glass is achieved by cutting facets out of colour "flashed" on one side of the glass.

Dungannon, Co Tyrone

Pictorial scenes in late Victorian houses often included painted portraits of allegorical figures.

Sans Souci Park, Belfast

Other popular subjects included birds and fruit, the latter particularly in dining rooms.

Castledawson, Co L'derry

Towards the end of the 19th century the influence of Art Nouveau was found in leaded glass in inglenooks.

Rosetta Park, Belfast

This narrow rosebush window in a bathroom of about 1900 uses obscured glass and even a bull's eye.

Annadale Avenue, Belfast (*above*)

Castledawson, Co L'derry (*left*)

In the early 20th century coloured leaded glass graced churches and homes alike with idyllic pictures of countryside and seascapes.

Hatton Drive, Belfast

Houses built between the wars often had leaded light upper panes and sheet glass below, combining ornament and utility.

Comber, Co Down

When houses didn't have enough ceiling height for a fanlight, a glazed front door let light in, often through a picture.

Lurgan, Co Armagh

An unusual Art Deco front door, with the stepped fanlight and geometrical pattern of coloured glass.

Antrim, Co Antrim

Acid-etching of glass provides privacy for pub windows and house doors, and can be used to advertise at the same time.

Church Street, Belfast

Less common was the use of coloured glass to provide privacy screens, usually framed independently of the window.

Malone Road, Belfast

Coloured glass was commonly used on the margins of staircase windows, often with flashed corner panes.

Armagh, Co Armagh

The white lettering on this glass ensures that the message can be read from outside as well as in.

Kilkeel, Co Down

Part of a magnificent frieze of period cars designed by local stained glass firm Clokey's about 1945, celebrating the days when it was a pleasure to take one's motor for a spin at the weekend.

Dormers

Once the Victorians had liberated the roof from the low pitches beloved of the Georgians it was only a matter of time before the roofspace would be properly inhabited, and although at first it was lit by a skylight or a small window in the gable, dormer windows soon appeared in brilliant profusion. Attics may have been the domain of servants and small children, but the dormer was a place where the builder could often give free rein to his architectural imagination.

For the sake of convenience, dormers are categorised here as wall dormers (in which the wall rises above the eaves to form the dormer) and roof dormers (of a lighter construction supported on the roof joists), although there is not necessarily a chronological progression from the one to the other.

Although bargeboards will be considered again in more detail later, there are plenty of examples to relish on the small scale of the dormer window, ranging from the plain to the almost over-ornate.

Hardcastle Street, Belfast

Streets of brick terraced housing were built at an enormous pace in late 19th century Belfast, each with its own vocabulary of decorative brickwork and very often with dormers like this.

Benburb, Co Tyrone

In its most vestigial form, the dormer may be little more than an indication that there is a door below it.

Coleraine, Co L'derry

This elaborate dormer is part of the ornament around the window but probably has little real function.

Bangor, Co Down

Like a submarine prowling below the eaves line this window probably has hidden heights inside.

Caledon, Co Tyrone

The elaborate apex board here indicates that there is a raised ceiling just below it.

Castlerock, Co L'derry

The window rises through the wallhead to become a genuine dormer, with a rather classical bracketed skew.

Cookstown, Co Tyrone

A sort of kangaroo dormer, with a tiny upper light just above the main dormer, possibly lighting a true attic.

Greyabbey, Co Down

Emerging from the roof as if lifting a lid on it, this catslide dormer makes a very discreet appearance.

Warrenpoint, Co Down

These dormers, on the other hand, are a lot taller than most, with bargeboards like a small hat fitted on a large head.

Bangor, Co Down

Bigger still, a pair of steep High Victorian gables with apex boards and finials forming a dramatic entrance.

Botanic Avenue, Belfast

An unusual barrel-roofed dormer with brick trim and lead covering - with some fine chimneys next door.

Coleraine, Co L'derry

A pair of rather stolid half-hipped dormers, probably dating from around 1900, with small-pane upper lights.

Coleraine, Co L'derry

The most common type of wallhead dormer is triangular, seen here in a simple form with a skew and finial.

Agincourt Avenue, Belfast

A plain triangular dormer with brick eaves and a terracotta finial, demonstrating the problem of gutters round such dormers.

Lisburn Road, Belfast

A simple but pretty bargeboard and finial over a round-headed window. Note the cockscomb ridge behind.

Dundonald, Co Down

A slightly steeper but more spacious dormer with frilly bargeboard, and again an ornamental ridge to the main roof.

Woodstock Road, Belfast

The bargeboard on this dormer recalls a particularly rough sea and is restrained by a finial and crossbar.

Cookstown, Co Tyrone

A bargeboard with an open apex board and quatrefoil over a pair of windows in stone surrounds, dated 1896.

Cookstown, Co Tyrone

Of very similar date, with leaded top lights in a mullioned window, complete with finial and drop finial.

Enniskillen, Co Fermanagh

An unusual bargeboard with a single tooth on each side, embracing a casement window.

Caledon, Co Tyrone

A particularly wide dormer over a tripartite window with very small upper panes, this has a series of teeth on the otherwise plain bargeboards, and appears never to have had a finial or decorative apex over the plain gable.

Coleraine, Co L'derry

A simple bargeboard over a roundheaded window, the composition focusing on the wrought-iron finial at its apex.

Rostrevor, Co Down

Heavily impressive with its scalloped overhanging eaves in clerical black, and fleur-de-lis ridge tiles, this dormer marks a parochial house. The windows themselves have serious quoinstone surrounds.

Gilford, Co Down

Warrenpoint, Co Down

Dyan, Co Tyrone

Rugby Avenue, Belfast

Cushendall, Co Antrim

Woodstock Road, Belfast

A selection of wallhead dormers, showing the variety possible from the adjustment of elements like roof pitch and bargeboard design. The Gilford example has a very simple bargeboard but substantial onion-topped finials; the Warrenpoint one an unusual fretted pattern of bargeboard; the Dyan one a pleasant deep eaves. The finials on the Rugby Avenue and Woodstock Road dormer are impressive, while the teeth below the Cushendall one and the frills on the Woodstock Road one create interesting shadows.

Bessbrook, Co Armagh

Aughnacloy, Co Tyrone

Newcastle, Co Down

Lisburn Road, Belfast

Lisburn Road, Belfast

Newtownards, Co Down

Bessbrook boasts some splendid bargeboards, several with the distinctive knobbly design here; the dormers at Aughnacloy and Newcastle are comparatively shallow-pitched, the former with a lovely wave-formation bargeboard. The bottom three dormers have round-headed windows, the middle one with a polychrome brick surround and a crossbar supporting the finial while the keystone to the Newtownards example bears a lump of ornamental plaster that might be heraldic or might be vegetable - it is the neat fretwork of the bargeboard that catches the eye.

Comber, Co Down

The sight of rows of tightly packed dormers painted in cheerful colours brightens even a grey day. In this case the round-headed windows are set in brick reveals as stone is harder to form; they may also be later additions to the building.

Comber, Co Down

An unusually tall round-headed dormer window whose bargeboard echoes the shape of the opening.

Lurgan, Co Armagh

More often, as here, the dormer gable is much larger than the window set into it.

Coleraine, Co L'derry

Coleraine, Co L'derry

Two dormers with segmental-headed windows and elaborate metal finials. Note the beard below the cill on the left and the way the flat plaster band round the right-hand window sets off the intricate eaves and bargeboard.

Newcastle, Co Down

An apex-boarded dormer with segmental window forming part of an ornate composition with the eaves board.

Warrenpoint, Co Down

Occasionally wallhead dormers have glass sides, to access the view from all directions and give a feeling of lightness to the design.

Benburb, Co Tyrone

Sometimes dormers take their place picturesquely alongside their big brothers the gables, in this case each with identical bargeboards and finials.

Warrenpoint, Co Down

Sometimes the big brother has far too much detail to squeeze onto a mere dormer and they become variations on a theme.

Downpatrick, Co Down   **Greyabbey, Co Down**

One of the problems with dormers is deciding how to run the rainwater off the roof past them. The usual solution is to take a short downpipe from each small section of gutter between the dormers down to a string course gutter either just below the dormer cills or *(right)* as a cill course. Occasionally, however, things do go wrong...

Ballyclare, Co Antrim   **Draperstown, Co L'derry**

The downpipe *(left)* starts off at the obvious position between the dormers, but instead of carrying on vertically, it swerves off to the left over the nice lettering. However, perhaps it is better than the alternative of running the gutter along the whole elevation, ignoring the presence of dormers *(right)*.

Ballyhalbert, Co Down

The simple shallow dormer marks the entrance of this three-bay house; giving character to an otherwise plain and quite vernacular building.

Lisburn, Co Antrim

Occasionally a bay window will run up through the eaves to form a dormer - in this case slate-clad and with a skirt of slates trimmed with exposed rafter ends.

Armagh, Co Armagh

More often, the bay window stops short of the dormer. This example has an apex board and flourishes at the eaves.

Coleraine, Co L'derry

A more typical example, but with a finial and very small panes at the top of the sash windows.

Bangor, Co Down

A strange hammer-headed dormer set over a bay. Where windows occur in gables, as here, they tend to be small.

Cromac Square, Belfast

A pair of windows marked by a brick gable and heraldic shield, combining brick and stucco to good effect.

Warrenpoint, Co Down

Two round-headed windows sharing a handsome dormer with fretted apex-board, brackets and a finial taller than the windows themselves. The brackets on the dormer nicely echo the corbels supporting the eaves.

Warrenpoint, Co Down

A simpler apex board with trefoil decoration over more basic but narrow windows.

Newcastle, Co Down

A very basic bargeboard to a rather shallow dormer, but enlivened by the tightly-packed window eyebrows.

Larne, Co Antrim

Another double dormer, this time with a diamond at the top of the dormer. Note the fully-glazed oriel window.

Newtownards, Co Down

Moving the dormer towards the roof, this gable has a segmental-headed pediment giving an Italianate appearance.

Royal Avenue, Belfast

These late Victorian pediments, looking like part of the wall but set above the cornice line, are topped with ball finials.

Surrey Street, Belfast

A very unusual triangular bay window topped by an even stranger dormer with a bargeboard like a ship's prow.

Derry, Co L'derry

This Edwardian dormer swithers between Baroque and Art Nouveau in style, making an exuberant roofline.

Bangor, Co Down

Rows of dormers are always much more than the sum of their parts, creating a rhythm across a terrace that is impossible in most individual buildings. This terrace with its Dutch dormers and row of complete chimneys makes a strong statement.

Hilden, Co Antrim

Whether through accident or design, the palette of warm colours employed on this terrace of houses works well.

Strabane, Co Tyrone

In contrast to the unpainted render of the building, the dormers, eaves and ironwork here make a brave statement in the morning sunlight.

Castleward, Co Down

Although other details have changed, the row of dormers are the single most important architectural feature of this cottage.

Rugby Avenue, Belfast

The first way of getting light through the roof was the skylight. Modern velux windows are larger but similar.

Newcastle, Co Down

More ornamental, though frankly less efficient, are small triangular rooflights like this one with its terracotta finial.

Rostrevor, Co Down

Very handsome, and more Gothic, set in its fishscale roof, but still not very illuminating.

Comber, Co Down

Newtownards, Co Down

Ballynahinch, Co Down

Here is the proper roof dormer, usually with a frilly bargeboard and finial, sometimes with glazed sides (*left*), sometimes with wavy bargeboards or round-headed windows (*centre*), sometimes comparatively sombre and modest (*right*). Although these rise in line with the face of the wall, the projected eaves make them look as if they are further up the roof.

Woodstock Road, Belfast

A small but elaborate bargeboard missing its finial but with cartwheel terminations and glazed sides.

Newtownards, Co Down

Because many roof dormers are constructed of timber they have to be painted, and can be more eye-catching than the lower windows. This building has traces of an earlier resident who sold boots.

Newry, Co Down

An extraordinarily ornate terrace which has chimneys and dormers to match its intricate doorcases.

Kilkeel, Co Down

This dormer has casement windows, suitable for flinging open on bright summer mornings.

Ballycastle, Co Antrim

The upper sash has a triangular top, to maximise daylight coming in to this dormer.

Bangor, Co Down

A catslide dormer with a side porthole, looking as if it could be folded back into the roof when not in use.

Armagh, Co Armagh

Dungannon, Co Tyrone

Glendower Street, Belfast

Side-glazed roof dormers, from the partially sheeted version on the left, only glazing the part with a useful view, through the Arts & Crafts dormer to the long but deep-eaved version *(right)*. The Dungannon dormer has a ridge tile that echoes its bargeboard.

Markethill, Co Armagh

Side-clad in slate to match the rest of the roof this dormer is almost camouflaged, and its window margin-paned.

Comber, Co Down

With the growing fashion for rosemary tiles around 1900, this dormer was given contrasting tiled cheeks.

Bangor, Co Down

A tall elegant glazed dormer with a shallow barrel roof making the most of the sea views.

Rostrevor, Co Down

A picturesque effect can sometimes be made from pairing a roof dormer with a similarly-detailed wall dormer, as here. The windows of the upper dormer (which is shared by two houses) are so small as to indicate that the effect is ornamental.

Bessbrook, Co Armagh

Dormers with this type of half-hipped roof are sometimes called bonnet dormers, and are common in Scotland.

Ormeau Avenue, Belfast

The projecting curved front roof of this dormer has the appearance of a schoolboy's cap.

Arthur Square, Belfast

Below this bellcast-roofed dormer is an arched outlet (as *above*) draining the parapet roof into the gutter.

Castlerock, Co L'derry

This terrace with its dozen dormers gracing a steeply-pitched roof was designed in 1892 and is known as the Twelve Apostles. The terracotta finials and cast-iron latticed windows are unusual and distinctive.

Dungannon, Co Tyrone

These lowering slate-clad dormers have the appearance of helmeted and chainmail-clad Norman soldiers assembled in formation.

Newry, Co Down

Above a heavily-corbelled eaves this half-hipped dormer with its finial provides a welcome spot of lightness between building and sky.

Armagh, Co Armagh

These wavy-roofed dormers (originally with leaded-light casements as on the right) probably date from about 1900.

Newcastle, Co Down

A complete bay window on the roof, with full-height windows, half-hipped roof and dentilled eaves.

Kilkeel, Co Down

Somewhat easier is to lay three windows in a row, and add ornamental side-cheeks, as here.

Lindsayville, Co Tyrone

One of the smallest windows under one of the largest roofs among all the dormers illustrated here.

Castle Place, Belfast

These dormers are attached to the sloping pitch of a mansard roof. The decoration including side cheeks and some abstract decoration in the pediments is quite idiosyncratic, while the faceted corbels below the eaves enrich the effect.

Craigavad, Co Down

A strange triangular-headed window set beneath a deep bargeboard decorated by knobbly branches.

Aughnacloy, Co Tyrone

Another dormer with elaborate side-cheeks, echoing the rhythm of the bargeboard.

Cushendun, Co Antrim

A picturesque cottage window, small pane casements opening out from the spacious attic behind the mansard roof.

Kilkeel, Co Down

A pretty pair of dormers with side-cheeks and matching bargeboards, glazed sides and casement windows whose proportion suits the slightly broader width of these dormers.

Ballygawley, Co Tyrone

A fully-glazed dormer with slender columns attached to the front supporting a plain pediment.

Cookstown, Co Tyrone

Pilasters on the front support kneelers at the corners of this dormer. A faceted block covers the junction of the finial.

Lisburn Road, Belfast

The joists supporting a roof are normally cut short or hidden at the eaves, but here are exposed as an ornamental feature.

Lurgan, Co Armagh

The "joist ends" to this fancy dormer are probably dummies, but the pediment has a rising sun motif and finial.

Enniskillen, Co Fermanagh

A simple fully-glazed dormer with a very intricately-fretted apex formed round a crosspiece and finial.

Draperstown, Co L'derry

A more recent dormer with paired brackets supporting the deep eaves on each side, and slate cladding.

Newtownards, Co Down

A typical roof dormer with handsome wrought-iron finial and neatly fretted bargeboard. The yellow brick chimney is not uncommon as it used a harder brick than that normally available locally.

85

Doors

Doors are as essential to buildings as taxes and death are inevitable in life, but although they serve the lowly function of giving access to whatever may lie inside they can be relished for their intrinsic elegance.

Although actual doors have to relate to the human scale (and presumably will evolve to greater heights with successively taller generations), it is often the surrounds that create the character of an opening, borrowing Classical or Gothic finery and dressing it with fanlights or sidelights to create something much grander.

The story of doors runs from the half door to various kinds of panelled doors, and includes the ways light can be let in through, over or beside them, and the ways they are grouped in terraces or round carriageways. Much of the history of a door can be found in its ironmongery (the knockers, letterplates, knobs, hinges and locks) which may be symbolic, modest or brash. Years of polishing brass letterplates create a patina that cannot be achieved from scratch.

Dundrum, Co Down

Most of the buildings in this book are in public streets. The noble but very sad ruin of Mount Panther is visible from the main road but set back considerably from it. However, these sidelights were too good to leave out.

87

Newcastle, Co Down

A pretty thatched cottage with the traditional half-door (to let light in and keep the children in and the hens out). Another function of the half door was to let in air to feed the fire, as early windows were often fixed and could not be opened.

Teemore, Co Fermanagh

Seen from the inside the common arrangement of a full door and an outer half door can be appreciated.

Ballycastle, Co Antrim

Another great function of the half door is that you can lean on it, as on a fence, to watch the world go by and chat to the neighbours. Notice the St Bridget's cross propped on the fanlight of the neighbouring door.

Broughshane, Co Antrim

The hinging arrangement for the inner and outer doors and the weatherboard over the half door are quite complex.

Ballydugan, Co Down

Most timber used in Ulster is softwood pine, but this barn has lintels of oak, now hard as iron.

Teemore, Co Fermanagh

Seamus Curry was born in this three-roomed cottage built of local clay and thatched with local rye straw, and must have been in and out of the half door many times a day for over seventy years.

Donaghmore, Co Down

An old door can be repaired many times before it is finally done, more patch than cloth.

Rostrevor, Co Down

The simplest form of door is sheeted, that is to say with vertical boards fixed to a stiffening frame. This door has a foxy brass knocker.

Dungannon, Co Tyrone

Door frames were often set on stones, as here, to prevent rising damp from rotting the posts.

Glenarm, Co Antrim

Traditionally a door might only have horizontal "ledges" to stiffen it. Diagonal braces were added to prevent warping.

Glenoe, Co Antrim

Internal doors were often very thin but didn't warp as timber was well seasoned. This door is about five feet high.

Glenarm, Co Antrim

More sophisticated buildings might have diagonal sheeting, set to throw water off as here.

Castleton Gardens, Belfast

Modern timber usually requires a perimeter frame as well as the traditional ledges and braces.

Markethill, Co Armagh

Although framed like a panel door, this lacks mouldings and the boarded panels are flush with the frame.

Newry, Co Down

Panel doors were more sophisticated than sheeted ones, and Georgian examples typically had six panels like this.

Enniskillen, Co Fermanagh

Untypically the upper and lower panels here are the same size and the corners are rather fussily blocked.

Albion Street, Belfast

There are many variations on two-panelled doors, the most common being as here with arched tops.

Enniskillen, Co Fermanagh

Here the panels are broken up by central roundels, and the fanlight has a typical spiderweb pattern.

Ballycastle, Co Antrim

Victorian panel doors usually had four panels with timber mouldings round them as here.

Little Victoria Street, Belfast

High Victorian mouldings could be quite substantial as here, often involving a mixture of square and scotia mouldings.

Sans Souci Park, Belfast

Sometimes the panels were "fielded" or faceted to give more feeling of depth and grandeur.

Cookstown, Co Tyrone

This very elaborate Victorian door has fielded panels decorated with filigree mouldings.

Eglantine Avenue, Belfast

A nine-panel door in an uncommon triple layout, with bold mouldings in a wide opening.

Malone Road, Belfast

Looking more closely at the mouldings on a mid-Victorian door the depth of the carving is apparent.

Hilden, Co Antrim

The cross pattern imposed on the upper panel of this door is unusual, as is the dogtooth brickwork over it.

Donegall Street, Belfast

Uniquely this parochial house has a brass door, lovingly polished over the decades to reflect passers-by. The house dates from about 1820 but the age of the door itself is not known.

Castlederg, Co Tyrone

Where a wide door has to open into a confined space a double door has neater leaves than a single one.

Tandragee, Co Armagh

Often double doors led into shops or warehouses, though the fanlight here suggests that this was always a house.

Fivemiletown, Co Tyrone

Another favourite feature of shops and pubs was the corner door, here set under a scrolled pediment.

Glenarm, Co Antrim **Glenarm, Co Antrim**

Since many houses had no windows into their halls there was a problem when half-doors were phased out, and the solution was fanlights - small windows just above the door. Since they weren't for looking through they could use small offcuts of poor quality glass, initially in a "mouth-organ" fashion echoing the small-pane sashes alongside.

Gracehill, Co Antrim

A late 18th century shop door with quite a handsome mouth-organ fanlight set under a stone soldier arch.

Glenarm, Co Antrim

A more sophisticated variant on the mouth-organ fanlight, with larger panes shaped into arches.

Caledon, Co Tyrone

Small panes could also be set out in a lozenge formation as here in mill housing at Caledon.

Newry, Co Down

Awkwardly placed over the handsome fielded door (which may be later?) is a more basic lozenge fanlight.

Armagh, Co Armagh

Fanlights can be formed from timber, cast iron, hoop iron or leadwork, deriving their strength from the timber frame. Here the combination of a double-circle and smaller circles set within lozenges is underlined by small bosses.

Glenarm, Co Antrim

A very simple fanlight formed of intersecting circles in this pedimented doorcase, again in Glenarm.

Dungannon, Co Tyrone

Apologies for the product placement in front of this handsome doorcase with its tulip-shaped capitals.

Greyabbey, Co Down

The knitted pattern of circles and semicircles in this fanlight under an aedicule catches the eye.

Glenarm, Co Antrim

A geometrical pattern formed from rectangles of glass, probably set between timber glazing bars.

Newtownbutler, Co Fermanagh

A whitewashed house with a bold fanlight with a large central lozenge over a double door with handsome big base stones, and a step raising the whole element well above the level of any ground water.

Dungannon, Co Tyrone

A Gibbsian doorcase whose blocks are echoed in the blocks of the geometrical fanlight.

Newtownbutler, Co Fermanagh

A wide but rather arbitrary fanlight above a splendid double door with corbels and pilasters.

Moneymore, Co L'derry

So much care was taken on the scooped surround that the designer seems not to have had time to work out the fanlight.

Glenarm, Co Antrim

The plain stone surround and four-panel door set off the elegant figure-of-eight pattern fanlight.

Dundonald, Co Down

A pointed Gothic arch with moulded Gothic tracery in its fanlight, always looking ecclesiastical or educational.

Bleary, Co Down

A thatched cottage with Gothic glazing in its round-headed fanlight, adding instant style.

Comber, Co Down

At first sight the fanlight in this broken pediment is Gothic too, but really it follows its own instinct.

Comber, Co Down

The simple spoke fanlight in a round-headed Ards doorcase is a classic combination.

Derry, Co L'derry

The same pattern of fanlight extended over a wider doorcase with moulded surround and columns either side of the door. When painted neatly, fanlights like these are very slim and barely obstruct the light at all.

Markethill, Co Armagh

Normally the centre of a spoke fanlight is a semicircle, but here it has been pulled into a petal shape.

Kircubbin, Co Down

A complex spoke pattern, set over an early door where the base panels are flush with the frame.

Cushendall, Co Antrim

Boldly painted quoins enclose this recessed porch with a sunburst pattern of spoke fanlight.

Comber, Co Down

The best-known fanlight pattern is the spiderweb, with the spokes linked by loops round the border.

Moy, Co Tyrone

In this more elaborate example fleurs-de-lis drop from each link and there is a circle of chains above the focal point.

Glenarm, Co Antrim

Lovely old glass in the fanlight of a round-headed doorcase, with the focal point raised to become an ellipse.

Saintfield, Co Down

A spiderweb fanlight extended over a pair of Ionic columns in this doorcase, which comes complete with bootscraper.

Saintfield, Co Down

Four pilasters terminate rather uncertainly below this shallow wide fanlight with sidelights.

Derry, Co L'derry

A tall, wide and handsome doorcase with elaborate spiderweb fanlight and pairs of corbelled pilasters.

Lisburn, Co Antrim

When the links between the spokes are inverted the more cheerful petal fanlight is produced. This is a particularly elaborate example, set in a deep portico and with fleurs-de-lis on the ends of decorated spokes.

Armagh, Co Armagh

A deep fanlight above a narrow door, with the spandrels of the rectangular fanlight filled with circles.

Newry, Co Down

A semicircular opening with a petal fanlight over the recessed Ionic columns, and steps up to the sheeted door.

Newry, Co Down

Bands of cut stone surround an unusual six-panel door three panels wide, with a shallow petal fanlight.

Newry, Co Down

A still shallower petal fanlight beneath a bracketed pediment enclosing the recessed doorcase with Doric columns.

Limavady, Co L'derry

A basic petal fanlight over a Greek key patterned cornice with Ionic columns below.

Derrygonnelly, Co Fermanagh

A red setter marches past a six-panel door with a petal fanlight of almost daisy-like simplicity. As is common in Fermanagh, the door frame is kept clear of the ground on large base stones.

Greyabbey, Co Down

A petal fanlight set inside the scoops of a spiderweb fanlight, creating lozenges at each junction.

Lisburn, Co Antrim

This kind of fanlight, with its drooping arcs, might be described as a bat's-wing. This version, set above a Doric entablature, has epaulettes of petal lobes on either side of the central oval.

Gracehill, Co Antrim

The pure bat's-wing, in a building from the middle of the 18th century, set in a plain round-headed surround.

Hamilton Street, Belfast

In contrast, these upwardly-curved lobes might be called peacock-tails. This pair of doors, with the narrow sheeted alleyway door between them, have fanlights built around hoop-iron formed inside a timber frame.

Moira, Co Down

A spread-out version of a peacock-tail fanlight in an unusual surround with paired Ionic columns and corbels.

Enniskillen, Co Fermanagh

Two variations on peacock fanlights at the handsome Willoughby Terrace in Enniskillen. Both have the original two-panel doors with central lozenges and Doric columns, but the fanlight on the left combines peacocks and bats.

Enniskillen, Co Fermanagh

A fanlight built around circles linked in a rather arbitrary manner. The door has been scumbled or "grained" with paint.

Warrenpoint, Co Down

A fanlight decorated with a big O. Note the unusual gate and the voussoirs in the plaster coursing round the opening.

Cromwell Road, Belfast

A hollowed-out pediment containing an elliptical light over the Ionic columns and Greek-key entablature.

Moneymore, Co L'derry

A symbolic fanlight at the entrance to a Masonic Hall, with the eye of God in the keystone.

Markethill, Co Armagh

Sometimes a fanlight isn't enough and small windows are required at either side of the doorcase to light the hall.

Cornabrass, Co Fermanagh

Mouth-organ sidelights as part of the doorcase in an abandoned vernacular building.

Downpatrick, Co Down

Sidelights and fanlight combined into one generous surround, complete with vet's brass signplate.

Portglenone, Co Antrim

A fielded door set in a segmental-headed framework of fanlight, sidelights and corner panes.

Donaghmore, Co Tyrone

Margin-paned sidelights beneath a feathery fanlight in an elliptical-headed recessed porch. Fresh limewash.

Ahoghill, Co Antrim

A boldly delineated quoined surround to a door with wide fanlight and curiously dense sidelights.

Rostrevor, Co Down

A smart six-panel door with matching fanlight and sidelights, granite cills and a pebble path.

Ballywalter, Co Down

Sidelights set between pairs of fluted pilasters support an elliptical fanlight. Perhaps the most unusual feature of this doorcase, however, is the door itself with variously proportioned panels and fans in the spandrels of the octagonal panels.

Lurgan, Co Armagh

A more formal doorcase. The fragment of railing was left for safety during the wartime stripping of iron.

Newtownards, Co Down

A door with straightforward fanlight and sidelights set under a segmental arch supported on pilasters.

Gracehill, Co Antrim

The pattern of arcs in the fanlight is echoed at a smaller scale in the sidelights.

Donaghadee, Co Down

The looped pattern in this fishing town fanlight is reminiscent of the knots made by sailors in rope.

Coalisland, Co Tyrone

Sometimes as here the need is felt to put net curtains behind the sidelights to maintain privacy.

Greyabbey, Co Down

Although a degree of privacy was created by using small pane sidelights, etched glass was preferred around 1890.

Comber, Co Down

With the Arts & Crafts movement at the end of the 19th century symmetry was no longer so important.

Comber, Co Down

Glenarm, Co Antrim

Comber, Co Down

For those who couldn't afford fanlights there was the option of cutting a hole in the sheeted door, either square (*left*) or circular (*right*). The door on the right has had repairs spliced in at the bottom of the sheeting where timber rots easily.

A purpose-made glazed door probably inserted into an earlier house about 1900.

Cushendun, Co Antrim

A deliberately picturesque Arts & Crafts door in a house of about 1930. Note the semicircular entrance step.

Palestine Street, Belfast

An unusually large and ornamental glazed opening with pilasters and ivy-clad arch.

Portrush, Co Antrim

Portrush has a number of distinctive doors like this from the turn of the last century.

Newry, Co Down

An asymmetrical rising sun motif in a glazed door of perhaps 1950. It is also echoed in the gate.

Comber, Co Down

A splendid shop door from about 1900, with glazed double doors set back from the shopfront behind a timber screen. The screen has a slightly raised pediment and dentil courses.

Warrenpoint, Co Down

A shop whose very name draws attention to the display of knitting patterns on its elegantly framed glazed door.

Ballycastle, Co Antrim

Another glazed shop door, with plate glass window and some carved wooden cresting over it.

Portrush, Co Antrim

A pedimented doorcase to a Masonic Hall. The swags below the pilaster capitals suggest a date about 1910.

Greyabbey, Co Down

A pair of etched glass doors with a pattern of fruit in an urn. The colour is unlikely to be original.

Rostrevor, Co Down

An intricate Gothic glazed door with pointed arch eyebrow terminating in female heads at either side.

Limavady, Co L'derry

A French door into the garden disguised as the central lower sash of a tripartite window, with folding base panels.

Bangor, Co Down

An Art Deco French door set in a steel semicircular window, complete with horizontal glazing bars.

Rosetta Park. Belfast

Geometrical stained glass like this was common around 1890, often incorporating small bulls' eyes.

Newtownards, Co Down

Donaghadee, Co Down

Pictorial stained glass is less common in doors, but sailing ships were popular designs in the 1930s (*left*) or more recently yachts (*right*). Both these examples incorporate white glass which is legible inside and outside.

Armagh, Co Armagh

Occasionally a fanlight can still be found that incorporates housing for a light (originally oil).

Ballycastle, Co Antrim

Before flagged pavements became common roads were muddy and steps helped to keep houses clean and dry.

Moy, Co Tyrone

In steep streets steps are necessary to access the doors but can take up much of the pavement.

Armagh, Co Armagh

A gracious flight of steps with railings up to a Georgian house in the cathedral city of Armagh.

Derry, Co L'derry

A massive flight of stone steps up to a couple of houses in an early Victorian terrace, wide enough to accommodate a coach and horses in some comfort. Pairing the houses makes a much greater impact than if they had had separate flights.

Portadown, Co Armagh

Greencastle, Co Tyrone

Farmhouses often had rooms alongside the house to accommodate cattle on the ground floor and hay on the first floor, which meant additional doors in the front elevation and a flight of steps up to the barn. In the left hand example the upper door has been converted to a window, and in the right hand example a further store is fitted under the stairs.

Enniskillen, Co Fermanagh

A simple carriageway door, often giving access to stabling at the rear of a group of houses.

Lisburn, Co Antrim

This door has a bold plinth and a slender moulding round the slightly curved opening.

Glenarm, Co Antrim

Rounded corners and big plaster quoins dignify this entrance. Note the decorative pavement.

Castlederg, Co Tyrone

Genuine stone quoins surround this entrance. The smaller wicket door inside the leaf gives entrance from the outside.

Newtownards, Co Down

This door has an arc-headed entrance, contrasting with the more common round-headed doorcase alongside.

Ballycastle, Co Antrim

The quoinstones and voussoirs are picked out here in contrasting colours from the wall.

Templepatrick, Co Antrim

Impressive iron hinges to a mock-Gothic gateway entrance. Working hinges are normally on the inside.

Warrenpoint, Co Down

An entrance with mock hinges and diagonal sheeting, set under a keystone and quoins.

Glenarm, Co Antrim

A dramatic piece of Walter Scott-ery, this barbican gateway has heavily rusticated stonework, lancet windows, fake hinges, a studded door and, most glorious, a fake portcullis ready to drop across the entrance.

Drumaness, Co Down   **Gilford, Co Down**   **Gracehill, Co Antrim**

Lisburn, Co Antrim   **Downpatrick, Co Down**   **Rostrevor, Co Down**

At the beginning of the 19th century most roads and footpaths were cobbled at best, and often little more than tracks through mud, with other flavours being added by passing horses and cows. Inevitably one's boots became dirty and scrapers were provided to remove the worst of the mire and clabber before entering the house. Even small terrace houses in towns had a suitable metal bar in an arched opening beside the door (*top left* and *centre*), while the freestanding pattern with knobs to grasp while scraping was found at grander houses. The introduction of cast iron enabled more elaborate examples to be produced in early Victorian times (*bottom centre* and *right*).

Cushendall, Co Antrim

A heavily fortified door two inches thick and sheeted with iron and studs for the village dungeon.

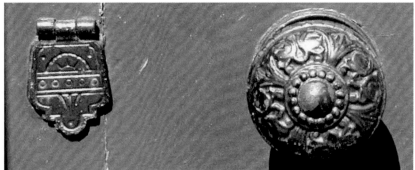

Enniskillen, Co Fermanagh

By contrast, one occasionally still sees a key left in the lock by a trusting pensioner (or a careless student).

(from top): **Lisburn, Co Antrim; Enniskillen, Co Fermanagh; Newry, Co Down**

Early door furniture tends to be iron, but there is a beautiful patina to be found on brass that has been polished over many years. Modern locks tend to be discreet, but Victorian lock covers or escutcheons (*top*) could be very elaborate.

Aughnacloy, Co Tyrone

This heavy iron ring-knocker dates from about 1850 and would have sounded through the almshouses.

Lisburn, Co Antrim

Lions are a common feature of knockers, fiercely defending the house and the iron ring.

Markethill, Co Armagh

This Georgian gentleman in a tricorn hat supports the knocker by a bolt through his head.

Ballycastle, Co Antrim

Camden Street, Belfast

Ballydugan, Co Antrim

Iron door knockers were often painted in with the door to protect them against rusting. As the pull ring became more elongated it metamorphosed into the teardrop (*left* and *centre*) or geometric style, and then became a solid iron knocker. In each case there is an iron boss on the door for the knocker to strike against.

Saintfield, Co Down

A lightly knotted design of knocker with a striking plate nearly as large as the knocker itself.

Lisburn, Co Antrim

A typical "doctor knocker", the design supposedly indicating the doctor's house.

Carnlough, Co Antrim

A mythological head and beaded knocker topped rather strangely with a ribbon bow.

Enniskillen, Co Fermanagh *(top left and bottom right)*; **Comber, Co Down** *(top right)*; and **Derry, Co L'derry**

Cast-iron letterplates were often ornate but quite small, as professional houses likely to receive substantial mail would have had a maid to receive it. Gradually it became unnecessary to describe the purpose of the aperture, and sometimes the knocker could be combined with the letterplate.

Enniskillen, Co Fermanagh　**Armagh, Co Armagh**　**Lisburn, Co Antrim**

This lovely brass bell (*left*) may have been adapted from a bell pull where the knob was pulled to ring a bell on a spring. After door pulls came clockwork bells, with the mechanism on the inside of the door. Some early electric bells were powered by battery rather than run power to the door.

Saintfield, Co Down

A whimsical piece of ironwork round the hinges of this church hall door, worthy of a fairty-tale castle.

Glenarm, Co Antrim

More fake hinges, enhancing a stable door between two romantic lancet windows.

Bradbury Place, Belfast

Modern door handles for a fish and chip shop, subtly advertising its product to passers-by.

Downpatrick, Co Down

It is considered lucky to put a found horseshoe over the door because iron repels evil spirits.

Portballintrae, Co Antrim

This owner is taking no chances, though there is no indication that the size of the shoe affects its power of catching luck.

Waringstown, Co Down

Normally the horseshoe is hung this way up to catch the luck, though some say it should be the other way to drop it in.

Enniskillen, Co Fermanagh

Probably dating from the 1930s, this brass door-knocker combines horse and shoe in one.

Corsale, Co Fermanagh

It's interesting to speculate whether this collection of brushes carries similar talismanic powers. Certainly the whitewash and thatch are immaculate, but the location is probably brought about by lack of storage space.

Porches

Adoor is often not enough to keep our wet and windy climate at bay, and an additional porch is often necessary, both to shelter the waiting visitor from rain and to keep the wind out of the house. Earlier buildings rarely had porches but they had become an integral part of many buildings by the end of the 19th century. As well as acting as a climate air-lock, they can store muddy boots and parcels ordered on the internet.

Before considering porches, however, there is the matter of the door surround, the frame in which a door is set that gives it increased significance or style. The possibility of using contrasting paint colours or materials adds to the liveliness or legibility of the elevation.

Armagh, Co Armagh

Actually the cow has nothing to do with this building, which is 18th century in date but with the handsome porch on dwarf colonettes probably added around 1870.

121

Comber, Co Down

A simple stone door surround, no more than a trim to the door opening with a rudimentary entablature.

Moy, Co Tyrone

A basic moulded surround rising to a broken pediment with a crest, adding a definite character to the plain door.

Donegall Street, Belfast

Somehow reminiscent of Downing Street, this scooped door surround dates from about 1830.

Rostrevor, Co Down

This doorcase certainly won't get lost. The sans-serif name is cast in with the plaster door surround.

Derry, Co L'derry

A High Victorian doorcase with staring roundels, the double doors probably leading to an inner porch.

Newry, Co Down

A very elaborate late Victorian doorcase with panels, colonettes, splayed base and intricate trimming.

Greyabbey, Co Down

The plain round-headed pilastered doorcase is known as an Ards doorcase, from its prevalence in the Ards area.

Newtownards, Co Down

This surround has a keystone bearing a swag of linen, pehaps indicating the trade of its builder.

Newtownards, Co Down

The Ards doorcase is often combined with Gibbsian blocks as here, making a lively streetscape.

Comber, Co Down

In this doorcase the mouldings of the pilaster terminate in a capital of upright fern leaves.

Greyabbey, Co Down

Patriotically painted in red and blue, this is another variation on the Ards door, with keystone and moulded head.

Antrim, Co Antrim

Of course the design was not unique to the Ards, and here it is found in Antrim with panelled pilasters.

Ballynahinch, Co Down

A shallow segmental-headed doorcase with buckles at the centre of each pilaster.

Glenallen Street, Belfast

Many of the Belfast streets cleared in the 1980s had imaginative ornament like these segmental labels over door and windows, executed in plaster and painted to contrast with the horizontal courses of the walls.

Clough, Co Down

This overgrown staircase and its doorcase with broad Ionic pilasters is all that remains of this Georgian house.

Gracehill, Co Antrim

A simple 18th century portico with almost detached fluted Ionic pilasters and a figure-of-eight fanlight.

Ballycastle, Co Antrim

A plain pilastered doorcase with four-panel door in a brightly painted shop-front.

Newtownards, Co Down

Fluted pilasters with rudimentary corbels and a keystone. Note the curtains to reduce sunlight into the hall.

Lurgan, Co Armagh

Leaves form a theme in this terrace, appearing in the two pediments and on the window keystone and corbels. Brackets supporting the window cills echo the capitals of the door pilasters.

Glenarm, Co Antrim

A Greek key pattern is hinted at on the pilasters to this doorcase with its figure-of-eight fanlight.

Newtownards, Co Down

Plain pilasters with neat Ionic-ish capitals contrast with the grained front door. The letterbox came after the doorknob.

Comber, Co Down

A fluted keystone and handsome version of Ionic capitals set off this stucco surround.

Downpatrick, Co Down

This 18th century doorcase has simple corbels supporting a rudimentary entablature.

Gilford, Co Down

Substantial decorative corbels support a rather insubstantial entablature, but do add dignity to the door.

Newry, Co Down

Getting bolder, there is a swag at the bottom of each pilaster, and a flower stuck jauntily above each corbel.

Glenarm, Co Antrim

Chunky early Victorian corbels support this entablature: simple, strong and elegant.

Lisburn Road, Belfast

The decorations at the corners of the entablature are the Greek pattern known as acroteria, here on a tiny pediment.

Enniskillen, Co Fermanagh

A stone-carved surround for the Savings Bank, with fluted pilasters and diamond-faceted capitals.

College Square North, Belfast

A pair of door surrounds of about 1830. That on the right with its fluted Ionic capitals, is more accurately Grecian, the other puts the components through an Italian Renaissance sieve.

Gracehill, Co Antrim

A Classical 18th century doorcase with fluted pilasters and dentilled entablature, to which is added a free carving of foliage.

Lisburn, Co Antrim

More vernacular, the fluted pilasters lead not to capitals or corbels but to a stamped floral pattern.

Ballynahinch, Co Down

The space between fanlight and entablature is heavily decorated, while the corbels carry faceted blocks.

Newry, Co Down

An eagle perched above an entablature precariously balanced on a couple of small colonettes.

Newtownards, Co Down　　　　　　　　　　**Hope Street, Belfast**

A pair of doorcases with bracketed entablatures: on the left the corbels lie outside the pilasters, emphasising the width of the door when there is no room to expand it upwards; on the right, the corbels are deeper and there is space for an arc of decoration over the entablature.

Newtownards, Co Down

An idiosyncratic paint scheme exaggerates the richness of the window heads and pilaster capitals with their fluted bases. Not content with carving one set of capitals at the door, the stonemason adds another set of horns on inner pilasters.

Upper Crescent, Belfast

A similar effect with a small colonette set inside a door surround, though here there is only the outline of a capital.

Lurgan, Co Armagh

Short columns on tall bases support the upper part of this surround. Note the frieze with dogtooths and rosettes.

Dungannon, Co Tyrone

With no attempt at Classical vocabulary, these iron brackets support the entablature as if it were a shelf.

Derry, Co L'derry

At the end of the 19th century eclecticism (meaning drawing on more or less everything for inspiration) became fashionable, and this free-hanging entablature with hints of Jacobean strapwork is a good example.

Glenanne, Co Armagh

A triple-decker door in a frame that has been moulded into a formal surround, set flush with the wall.

Derry, Co L'derry

A generous opening able to accommodate slender columns either side of the six-panel door.

Newtownards, Co Down

A handsome doorcase with a boot-scraper on each side to cope with the usual queue.

Ballynahinch, Co Down

A smartly grained four-panel door with central beaded divide in a surround recessed from the wall face.

Dublin Road, Belfast

Corinthian capitals on columns that support a brick arch with a stone keystone. Formerly Dr Scarlett's surgery.

Portglenone, Co Antrim

A very simply recessed door in a round-headed opening with deep reveals and thin outer moulding.

Lisburn, Co Antrim

Detail of a recessed portico with the full panoply of a Greek temple - fluted columns, metopes and triglyphs (representing joist ends when the Greeks had built in wood) and on the underside of the entablature mutules (like rows of pegs).

Downpatrick, Co Down

A thin but formal surround with attached fluted pilasters, dentilled frieze and a doubly symmetrical door.

Glenarm, Co Antrim

Clustered columns make up the supporting pilasters for this portico with its gilded lettering.

Ballycastle, Co Antrim

The columns of this portico look rather slender for their purpose - but perhaps it is the lettering that is heavy.

Newtownards, Co Down

Another Masonic entrance, laden with symbolism as usual, including sun, moon and compasses.

Galgorm, Co Antrim

A schoolhouse of 1878, built in the approved Gothic style into which it is hard to fit a door.

Dungannon, Co Tyrone

Gothic adapted for a terrace of High Victorian houses - trefoil fanlights set in Gothic arches.

Articlave, Co L'derry

A charming doorcase, with orange lilies painted on the two capitals, and frilly eaves overhead.

Armagh, Co Armagh

An elegant doorcase of about 1730 with Gibbsian doorcase (blocked quoinstones) and Gothic fanlight.

Ballyskeagh, Co Down

A Gibbsian doorcase of 1760, with stepped voussoirs over the flat arch, the cut stones contrasting with rubble walls.

Clogher, Co Tyrone

Rather like a periwig round the face of the modern door, this quaintly blocked Gibbsian doorcase is dated 1780.

Ballynahinch, Co Antrim

Polychrome brickwork opened the same possibilities for framing doors as for windows (*see* p.37).

Drumaness, Co Down

An unusual use of blue engineering brick to form elongated arches for a pair of doors.

Linenhall Street, Belfast

Brick and red sandstone together could make very handsome doorcases for the great Victorian linen warehouses.

The Mount, Belfast

There is an almost Moorish exuberance to this 1896 doorcase incorporating granite pilasters and terracotta plaques.

Enniskillen, Co Fermanagh

An Art Deco surround with a frieze of roundels and fluting and neo-Georgian geometrical fanlight.

Dungannon, Co Tyrone

Looking like an air-lock, this 1930s porch has octagonal windows and chamfered corners to the doorcase.

Portrush, Co Antrim

A frieze of young plants sprouting under the eaves of this stucco door surround, with more plants at the capitals. Victorian mass-produced plaster made such decoration possible at very affordable prices.

College Green, Belfast

This leafy decoration is probably carved into the sandstone of the Gothic lintel rather than cast as with plaster.

Derry, Co L'derry

An owl and a phoenix emerging, wings outstretched, from bundles of ferns look in better condition than the stone entablature they are supporting. For all their bravado, the birds look comic rather than impressive.

Florenceville Avenue, Belfast

An extraordinary surround, with Ionic capitals emerging from the wilderness at either end of the entablature.

134

Belleek, Co Fermanagh

A bold motif of circles on blocks in an otherwise plain elevation. This building probably originally had a thatched roof.

Groomsport, Co Down

On either side of the door plants climb up from a sort of flower pot, then under the balcony are much larger leaves.

Bangor, Co Down

This yacht club was built about 1900, and its initials are woven into a length of carved rope over the front door.

Albertbridge Road, Belfast

A surround with various bits of strapwork decoration, a bracketed entablature and eyebrow taking over from quoins.

Bundoran, Co Donegal

Part of a whole elevation decorated with coloured and varnished shells set into the plaster like a mosaic.

Newtownards, Co Down

Although the surround itself is not so exotic, the painted decoration of birds and plants looks central European.

Albion Street, Belfast

A pair of panel doors sharing a rather grand portico with swags of fruit at each corbel.

Newtownards, Co Down

The arrangement of house doors either side of a central carriageway door is common in terraces. Behind this terrace are stables that would probably have housed ponies and traps.

Lurgan, Co Armagh

These two doors are recessed inside a round-headed surround that looks to be carved out of the wall.

Penrose Street, Belfast

A pair of houses with porches set into the walls and round-headed arches with Corinthian capitals.

Newry, Co Down

Newry is particularly rich in doors grouped round carriageways, whether the conventional one above (but with granite surrounds and dividing railings) or the lower one with its flights of steps and correspondingly tall carriage door.

Rostrevor, Co Down

The unifying graining of house and yard doors doesn't disguise their very different characters.

Ballinderry, Co Antrim

In thatched cottages it was possible to have a low door in a shallow porch and take it in under the thick thatch roof without having to change pitches.

Charlemont, Co Armagh

Although now roofed in tin, this cottage was almost certainly thatched when the porch was built, and the decoration to it and the windows would look at home under thatch.

Mullylusty, Co Fermanagh

The traditional outshot porch with the thatch neatly covering and weathering in the projection.

Charlemont, Co Armagh

A house fit for a sherriff, with lone stars and a rising sun motif. Probably originally thatched, upgraded c1950.

Portavogie, Co Down

This has a minimalist modern look, but the plaster decoration would not look out of place on a much older house.

Rosslea, Co Fermanagh

The shallowness of this porch suggests that the house was originally a single-storey thatched cottage "riz up" into a second storey. Once the thatch has gone it is possible to provide a gable to the porch and roof it differently.

Killyman, Co Tyrone

Thinner and harder roofing materials like slate (or tin) dictated different roofing patterns like gabled porches.

Markethill, Co Armagh

This house was certainly thatched in 1900 and the bargeboard added to a previously flat porch in 1917.

Killyman, Co Tyrone

The combination of shallow porch and tin roof again suggests it was previously thatched.

Markethill, Co Armagh

The shallow pitch of this gable allows its ridge to fit under the main eaves without complex flashings.

Benburb, Co Tyrone

A crisp very upright little porch, one man wide and with a shock of coxcomb ridge standing to attention.

Charlemont, Co Armagh

In parts of Armagh and Tyrone there is a strong tradition of decorating walls and porches with pebbles, this being a neat but comparatively restrained example. As with earlier examples, the porch has been extended from an outshot into a gable.

Coalisland, Co Tyrone

This row of identical porches each with its finial, front door and side windows is like a line of sentryboxes.

Charlemont, Co Armagh

Another shallow porch, this time decorated with Masonic symbols suggesting its occupant was a member.

Helen's Bay, Co Down

A tall porch, constrained by the window above but probably designed as part of a two-storey building.

Killyman, Co Tyrone

This porch has been added onto an already-slated cottage, although the heavy mouldings on the door suggest that it may have been promoted to the porch from an earlier position in the building, perhaps the original front door.

Newtownbutler, Co Fermanagh

A hard one to date with its shallow pitched roof, wide opening and distinctive teardrop bargeboard.

Templemore Avenue, Belfast

An unusual elevation for a porch, with triple arches for door and windows, and the shield with room for a monogram.

Crawfordsburn, Co Down

A lean-to porch in front of a gingerbread Gothick cottage, complete with pointed arches and false hinges.

Dungannon, Co Tyrone

This porch looks like an add-on, with the door at the side to maximise head-room without affecting the window above.

Bellanaleck, Co Fermanagh

Another lone star porch, this looks like a complete rebuild rather than an adaptation of an earlier outshot.

Comber, Co Down

The paired windows on the front of this side-entry porch suggest that it serves two neighbouring houses.

Newry, Co Down

A rather grander porch with handsome bargeboard and round-headed window. Now used as a church.

Newcastle, Co Down

An exciting suite of porch and dormers, with the same frilly eaves-board and brackets unifying the main roof and the roofs of dormers and porch. The side entry to the porch may have been chosen for privacy.

Bangor, Co Down

A porch created at the front corner of a house built about 1930. The single column is striped with pebbles.

Antrim, Co Antrim

An idiosyncratic building with a horseshoe-shaped opening suggesting that its owner shoes horses. No longer of course, and a new recessed door has been put in place to keep out the draughts.

Downpatrick, Co Down

The recessed doorcase leading into an internal porch gives the building a feeling of depth.

Comber, Co Down

A porch without walls is mainly decorative, but it does serve to keep some of the rain off waiting visitors.

Benburb, Co Tyrone

The bargeboard and finial on this little porch do much to enliven an otherwise plain elevation.

Newcastle, Co Down

The real porch is behind the façade, this elaborate porch with its kneelers and finial is just to mark the front door.

Dungannon, Co Tyrone

Canvassers would need their umbrella while waiting at this door, but they could admire the bold simple lines of the bargeboard of this open porch.

Whiteabbey, Co Antrim

Built about 1900 for the Whiteabbey Flax Spinning Co, whose monogram is in the fretted cheeks of the porches, the eaves is reminiscent of railway architecture.

Holywood, Co Down

An unusual open porch with curved plan and iron railings along its parapet, probably added onto a plainer house of about 1850.

Armagh, Co Armagh

This unique porch with its clustered columns and freely carved pediment, looking a bit like a chaise longue on particularly tall legs, was planted onto an otherwise plain Georgian house.

Warrenpoint, Co Down

More permanent than most, this trellis porch has coloured glass windows at the sides.

Newtownbutler, Co Fermanagh

One up from the open porch was to add trellis walls, providing a sense of enclosure for imaginative visitors and a structure for rambling roses to climb up. The original doorcase with its moulded surround can be seen behind the trelliswork.

Clough, Co Down

A delightfully modest little trellis porch with a trim and delicate bargeboard; no need to pick out contrasting colours.

Newtownards, Co Down

As open as trelliswork but more structural, this porch is on a much larger scale and supports a substantial roof.

Bangor, Co Down

A verandah is an open porch you can sit in, often railed, which is often found on bungalows like this from about 1930.

Dungannon, Co Tyrone

Part of an Arts & Crafts house of about 1890 which has this split-level verandah and specially turned pillars.

Ormeau Road, Belfast

A handsome verandah with quatrefoils in the cornice as a corner porch for a house of about 1890.

Middletown, Co Armagh

This extraordinary structure has an almost Egyptian appearance with its striped columns.

Bangor, Co Down

A special order of architecture was devised for the columns on this otherwise quite plain house.

Newcastle, Co Down

It's hard to tell where this porch stops and becomes rooms as it could almost be a porch with glazed sides.

Downpatrick, Co Down

Glazed on all sides and with a pepper-pot roof terminating in a little iron crow's nest.

Coleraine, Co L'derry

Half-way to being a conservatory, this porch has an open area with cast-iron spandrels and a glazed portion.

Annadale Avenue, Belfast

For houses set in their own grounds rather than on the street, privacy was less important than ostentation. This glazed porch uses carved timbers, stained glass and iron cresting.

Cushendall, Co Antrim

A romantic mock-mediaeval porch of about 1900 with leaded windows and a half-timbered gable as the entrance to a stone church.

Markethill, Co Armagh

Neo-Norman to the last detail, including battlements, machicolations and a portcullis - Gosford Castle.

Newcastle, Co Down

Mid-Victorian architects would have looked to pattern books with drawings of mediaeval buidings for this.

Tudor Place, Belfast

A building in the Tudor style, as befitted its location, with square labels over windows and the Tudor arch eyebrow over the door terminating in bosses of mediaeval heads. The bargeboard, however, is too simple (see *left* for a more accurate version).

Newcastle, Co Down

Not really belonging to any particular style, but with an appearance halfway between Gothic and punk.

Cliftonville Road, Belfast

A Greek Revival porch of about 1830, complete with square outer pillars and fluted inner ones.

Comber, Co Down

A freer version of the same idea, much shallower and with wreaths and acroteria marking the column positions.

Portaferry, Co Down

Where better could you put your shop name than on a Classical portico over the Ionic capitals?

Lurgan, Co Armagh

Bengal Place, a terrace with channelled ground floor and Classical porticoes, being demolished in 1981. As well as the fluted columns the porticoes carried Greek key decoration, and the bossed railings were closely packed.

Armagh, Co Armagh

Small colonettes like this do not occur in Classical Greek architecture, but were very popular in Victorian times.

Botanic Avenue, Belfast

A Corinthian column supporting a shallow carved stone hood over a door with leaded fanlight.

Rostrevor, Co Down

A Gothic porch in timber and slate, full of carved detail, its roof shape echoed in the triangular roof dormer.

Ballynahinch, Co Down

When a doorcase is set forward like this the porch can rise to a dormer window, the whole unified by quoins.

Newcastle, Co Down

Actually a balcony more than a porch, this example shows how difficult it can be to categorise these details.

Warrenpoint, Co Down

A covered-in porch with generous windows and iron cresting on top by way of balustrading.

Armagh, Co Armagh

A bold canopy dating from about 1900 and welcoming customers with open arms.

Newcastle, Co Down

A glazed porch with barrel roof and leaded lights, providing an eye-catching entrance.

Portaferry, Co Down

Most details fall into one category or another, but this one defies classification. The chamfered brickwork and terracotta "capitals" are conventional enough, but then comes the stained glass with its flowery surround and the inner eyelid below it.

Bessbrook, Co Armagh

A nice pair of dripping bargeboards. The problem with semis of course is differences of opinion - while you hang your washing out and like the old plaster architraves, your neighbour has dumped the old windows and tidied up his porch.

Finaghy, Co Antrim

Big stone houses of the late 19th century often conceal warm varnished timber in their porches and halls.

Carnalea, Co Down

The period from about 1880 to 1910 saw an amazing variety of styles being explored, and often mixed together. This porch has a wavy Art Nouveau top but its effect depends on other irregular features, and of course on the palm trees.

Newcastle, Co Down

If you have green fingers and your house doesn't have a porch, you may have time to grow your own.

Roofs

It is easy to take roofs for granted. They are high above our heads and often difficult to see; they have rather uniform surfaces that are mostly flat; and in Georgian times architects tried to hide them altogether. They came into their own again when the Victorians introduced steeper-pitched roofs and taller chimneys.

At all times of course the roofs were essential for sheltering the quarters below from rain, channelling it down along valleys to gutters and hence to the ground without getting the walls wet. (Thatched cottages are the exception, the eaves being so deep that rain just drips from them without a gutter).

One of the surprising things about roofs is how big everything is up there - the roof is as big as the whole plan of the house, chimney pots can be shoulder-high, and if you laid all the bricks in an average chimney out end-to-end in a line they would cover a remarkable distance.

Teemore, Co Fermanagh

There can be few building materials as attractive as freshly laid thatch. From the soft organic shape of the roof to the neatly-trimmed ends of straw and the hazel withys that are set to pin the straws in place, the roof is natural and local.

155

Lisburn Road, Belfast

A typical Ulster roof is pitched at about 40° front and back, with gables at each end, usually with chimneys at the ridge.

Bangor, Co Down

In Georgian times (and again in the 1930s) roofs were often pitched at each side to form a hipped roof.

Belleek, Co Fermanagh

One of the standard designs for rural workers' cottages included the use of a half-hipped roof.

Randalstown, Co Antrim

On a grander scale the half-hip can create an interesting gable. Here the corbelled-out deep eaves create interesting shadows across the gable.

Cushendun, Co Antrim

The double-pitched mansard roof gets its name from a French Renaissance architect and ensures extra headroom in the attic. This example is slated with greenish Westmoreland slates.

Castlerock, Co L'derry

A simple way of covering an extension at the back of a house is a catslide roof that carries the pitch on down.

Coleraine, Co L'derry

Hoist roofs occur over loading bays of warehouses, sheltering the block and tackle for lifting goods up.

Glenanne, Co Armagh

The curious rounded gable so unsuitable for slate suggests that this house was formerly thatched.

Bangor, Co Down

Apart from lead ones, flat roofs were never found before the 20th century, because it was expected to rain.

Garvery, Co Fermanagh

Waringstown, Co Armagh

Beneath a thatch roof is a structure of tree-trunk purlins spanning from gable to gable. The depth of the thatch can be gauged from the chimney *(left)*. The internal surface of the roof was formed of turfs supported on branches.

157

Teemore, Co Fermanagh

In a few, mostly mud-walled, cottages the purlins are supported by cruck trusses transferring the roof load to the ground.

Moneymore, Co L'derry

A sophisticated 17th century timber roof with oak joists spanning between massive beams.

Downpatrick, Co Down

Much more common is the arrangement of a single purlin spanning between gables and rafters from eaves to ridge.

Newtownabbey, Co Antrim

Iron blocks like this were sometimes used in the 19th century to create more complex roof structures.

Cushendun, Co Antrim

Church roofs often show off the structure that is hidden in most domestic buildings - here a collar roof.

Lenaderg, Co Down

Part of a "Belfast roof truss", using light timbers to span wide areas under a shallow barrel roof.

Florencecourt, Co Fermanagh

In 1950 there were some 30,000 thatched cottages in Northern Ireland. That number has dwindled to about 300, many of which are now at risk. At one time a gabled thatch roof like this would have been a common sight.

Galgorm, Co Antrim

An unusual example of a comparatively urban thatched cottage; this also has a steep roof pitch with a substantial attic floor.

Bellarena, Co L'derry

On the North coast the thatch is sometimes executed in marram grass rather than straw, but almost always the thatch is tied down with ropes to counteract the strong winds.

Annalong, Co Down

Traditionally cottages are extended sideways, and sometimes the new building will be slated, retaining thatch on the original part.

Teemore, Co Fermanagh

Stooks of rye gathered for use in thatching. Note the "legs" keeping them off the ground, and the scarecrow. Thatchers would have grown their own straw to ensure good stalks.

Teemore, Co Fermanagh

Frank Gilligan laying a new layer of thatch and smoothing it off with the comb. Usually only the top layer of thatch is replaced and the innermost layer can be quite historic.

Annalong, Co Down

Corrugated iron (known as tin) was commonly used to replace thatch as it was lightweight, cheap and durable.

Greyabbey, Co Down

By far the most common roofing material here are the slates known as "Bangor Blues", imported from Bangor in Wales.

Markethill, Co Armagh

Occasionally agricultural buildings are found where the slates have been spaced out to make them go further.

Kiltonga, Co Down

This roof has small and irregular grey slates from Tullycavey near Ballywalter. They were often bedded in mortar.

Ballymone, Co Donegal

When using irregular slates it was often important to lay a graduated roof, with big slates rising to small ridge ones.

Cookstown, Co Tyrone

The Victorians enjoyed mixing slates of different colours and styles across a roof in mediaeval style.

Newmills, Co Tyrone

Sometimes slates could be cut into a "fishscale" shape for more ornamental effect. Such details were very popular in gate lodges where a lot had to be said in a small space on a small budget.

Sion Mills, Co Tyrone

Rosemary tiles are not common here, but were sometimes used to evoke a rustic simplicity or nostalgia. They are often hung on battens rather than nailed like slates.

Kilmood, Co Down

A quirky Gothick building with an exaggeratedly tall crowstep gable and lantern.

Ballymena, Co Antrim

A Scottish baronial lodge with what is known in Scotland as a corbie-step gable - though I've yet to see a crow on one.

Ballycastle, Co Antrim

When a gable terminates with flat slabs of stone at the gable they are supported on a skewstone.

Dungannon, Co Tyrone

This carved head looks like a skewstone although it has only a decorative function.

Edentrillick, Co Down

There are many variations on gables with a half-timbered effect, imitating English timber-framed buildings.

Dungannon, Co Tyrone

Sometimes the source material has been almost completely forgotten in a lilac haze.

Lurgan, Co Armagh

Sometimes bay windows are carried up into gables at the roof, often as here with half-timbering and kneelers.

Newcastle, Co Down

This gable is larger than the bay that supports it, like a rather portly cuckoo on a very plain nest.

Newcastle, Co Down

Unusually, this bay window actually morphs into the gable, creating a complex piece of roof.

Marlacoo, Co Armagh

A rising sun motif was popular in the 1930s, here combined with ball finials and a shouldered gable.

Lisburn Road, Belfast

Bangor, Co Down

At the end of the 19th century there was a vogue for gabled brick fronts, derived from Dutch urban architecture of the 17th century. Note the tumbled brickwork (laid diagonally, *left*) and the bulls' eyes (*right*).

163

Richhill, Co Armagh   **Lurgan, Co Armagh**   **Lisburn Road, Belfast**

The earliest example of a Dutch gable in Ulster dates from the late 17th century (*left*), but the same arrangement of a Baroque gable topped by a triangular pediment is found much later when the style was revived at the end of the 19th century, often as part of a more complex building.

The Mount, Belfast   **Bangor, Co Down**   **Newcastle, Co Down**

There is an overlap between gables and dormers, and these could as easily have been put amongst the dormers considered earlier, but stylistically they relate to the fully-fledged Dutch gables above. The one on the left shows a slight Moorish influence, the central one is a classic Dutch gable, while the one on the right is somewhat gauche.

164

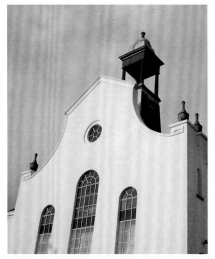

Rugby Road, Belfast

Unlike most of the details in this book, this is by a well-known architect, Clough Williams-Ellis, in the 1930s.

Lisburn Road, Belfast

This gable is a bit like a film set, quite impressive from one angle but looking cardboardy from another.

Belcoo, Co Fermanagh

Picking up the Art Deco theme, garages streamlined themselves with fancy gables in the 1930s.

Ballycastle, Co Antrim

Ballycastle, Co Antrim

Quite why garages should have plumped for Baroque gables isn't clear; but that other Modernist building type, the cinema, often started similarly with flowery gables tacked on to rather basic warehouses. Like garages, they developed from the neo-Classical (*left*, dated 1922) into hard-edged stepped gables (*right*).

Dundrum, Co Down

Some early roof ridges were carved from stone, particularly soft red sandstone as here.

Castlerock, Co L'derry

Much more common are red clay ridges, either plain or ornamented with crestings and finials.

Fivemiletown, Co Tyrone

Sometimes there is a nice echo between the ridge tiles and the chimney pots, as here.

Downpatrick, Co Down

The classic design for clay ridge tiles is the coxcomb, although there are many other variations.

Dundonald, Co Down

A finely stepped profile to these ridge tiles hints of Art Deco; the rustic brick in the chimney is also about 1930.

Newcastle, Co Down

An uncommon clay ridge tile with a spirited finial. Also unusual are the gable tile-hanging and corner acroterion.

Saintfield, Co Down

Some ridge tiles were made to accommodate a variety of insert crests, here fleurs-de-lis.

Lisburn Road, Belfast

Some ridge tiles always get broken somehow - due to carelessness either by ridge ladders or by speeding birds.

Botanic Gardens, Belfast

Iron flowers appropriately parade along the ridge of the Palm House, while iron crests top the university roof beyond.

Coleraine, Co L'derry

Even though most greenhouses are built of timber, the ornamental ridge is often of iron.

Limavady, Co L'derry

Lead is the common material for ridges and hips on shallow-pitched Georgian roofs. Note the short lengths used.

Ballynahinch, Co Down

In steep roofs such as on turrets it can be possible to hide the necessary lead flashings under the slates.

Larne, Co Antrim

It is a different world on top of a late Victorian house, with its wealth of chimneys, each bristling with tall pots. The ground seems very far below, and the sheer size of everything is surprising, but necessary to look in proportion at ground level.

Seaforde, Co Down

This granite chimney is quite low as its design is late Georgian, and originally it would not have had pots.

Enniskillen, Co Fermanagh

Chimneys and towers create a lively and interesting skyline, even though plumes of smoke are now a rare sight.

Walnut Court, Belfast

A fairly typical tall corbelled brick chimney with clay pots; and in the background an industrial chimney.

Ballynahinch, Co Down

In isolation tall chimneys can seem quite precarious, but they are usually several flues deep, giving stiffness.

The Mount, Belfast

The Mount, Belfast

The sheer number of flues in a Victorian house (almost one per room) required substantial chimneys, here decorated with vertical ribbing (*left*) or corbelled out on a decorative plinth (*right*).

Kircubbin, Co Down

An unusual elevation dominated by the chimney breast, like a medicine bottle set into the plasterwork.

Bangor, Co Down

Many tall stacks on front elevations like this have been removed, but in Victorian times they could be very grand.

Bangor, Co Down

A rounded boiler chimney on a church, executed in red sandstone, rather more attractive than most modern flues.

Lindsayville, Co Tyrone

A pair of aspiring octagonal chimneys rising from a common plinth. This kind of detail was common in estate houses.

Richhill, Co Armagh

Very early chimneys - the pots and their haunching being added later when coal fires superseded blazing logs.

Glenarm, Co Antrim

The Victorian roofline was dominated by tall chimneys, and by separating the individual chimneys on this stack a more complex effect could be created while still benefiting structurally from the contiguous flues.

University Square, Belfast

When only four flues were involved but a grand effect was still required, drastic measures had to be taken.

Malone Road, Belfast

The complexity of a chimney stack can be appreciated in this eight-decker seen at close quarters.

Rosetta Avenue, Belfast

A late Victorian multiple stack, very tall with corbelled tops and terracotta decoration.

Dungannon, Co Tyrone

Multiple stacks were often based on Elizabethan almshouses, but the model here seems to have been Tudor palaces.

Comber, Co Down

Sometimes chimney stacks can't be combined into thicker stacks and can only be linked together for support.

Lurgan, Co Armagh

The four chimney stalks here would have been very slender individually, but linked make a strong statement.

Ballycastle, Co Antrim

Classicists could be very coy about their chimneys, pushing them aside while dummies took pride of place.

Enniskillen, Co Fermanagh

The archetypal Victorian chimney pot, octagonal and usually with heart-shaped perforations under the rim.

Lisburn Road, Belfast

Before the Victorian period pots were less common and slate or brick divisions were placed between the flues.

Dungannon, Co Tyrone

One early design of chimney pot was this "dragon's tooth" type. The space rocket is of course 20th century.

Castlerock, Co L'derry

Four lovely calm classical pots like a row of columns left from some temple overlooking the sea.

Craigavad, Co Down

A magnificent collection of tapestried neo-Tudor chimney pots, like serried ranks of soldiers.

Stranmillis Road, Belfast

An expression of concern from the denizens of a flat without a chimney, and no way of letting Santa in.

Drains Bay, Co Antrim

At first sight like slender chimneys, but boldly going where no chimney can go, stone finials ornament many gables.

Glenarm, Co Antrim

This finial has suffered from its isolated position and the stone is foliating and flaking off.

Antrim, Co Antrim

This church of 1867 is greatly enhanced by the tall finial with its capital and chimney-like capping.

University Road, Belfast

Sometimes finials were put on the shoulders of gables rather than the peak, and this one is octagonal.

Tullyhogue, Co Tyrone

At the end of many crested ridges comes a terracotta finial, sometimes vertical like this, sometimes more Baroque.

Castledawson, Co L'derry

More of a trademark than a finial - Astley Brook & Co of Huddersfield made "fireproof garages" in the 1930s.

Mowhan, Co Armagh

Corn mills, like oast houses, required ventilators that could adjust to the wind, sometimes on turntables.

Moy, Co Tyrone

An elegant ventilator disguised to look like a dormer placed at the end of the roof ridge.

Bangor, Co Down

A belfry and weathercock (or rather ship-cock) on top of a castellated Arts & Crafts tower of 1905.

Lower Garfield Street, Belfast

A ventilator or lantern with very tall finial nestling amongst the chimneys above this group of buildings.

Sion Mills, Co Tyrone

A belfry and clock tower of about 1885, its skeleton cruelly exposed here but still dignified.

University Square, Belfast

A wonderful octagonal flight of fancy by WH Lynn, complete with arcading, finials, quatrefoils and gablets.

174

Killyleagh, Co Down

Round towers are famous ancient Irish relics, but this one is a Victorian addition to a Plantation castle.

Portrush, Co Antrim

A Scottish Baronial style building of 1870, with a round tower staircase. The complex roof plan is typical of picturesque Victorian designs.

Bangor, Co Down

One of the flanking towers of the former Grand Hotel, linked to another by cast-iron balconies.

College Gardens, Belfast

A romantic gate lodge by John Lanyon, its witch's hat turret echoed by the nearby gate pillar (in silhouette).

Alfred Street, Belfast

An ambitiously designed church with mock castellations and octagonal turrets framing the local dark red brick. St Malachy's is particularly remarkable for its fan-vaulted ceiling and intricately carved altar.

Donegall Square West, Belfast

Victoria Street, Belfast

Most of the sculpture on the Albert Memorial, Belfast's best-known leaning tower, had been removed for health and safety reasons but it has been painstakingly restored in recent years.

Royal Avenue, Belfast

Copper-clad domes on Italianate buildings of about 1890 punctuate the streetscape of Belfast.

Shankill Road, Belfast

Sometimes quite a small belfry can add a great deal to an otherwise modest building.

Derry, Co L'derry

A remarkable Art Nouveau department store from the end of the 19th century, with broken pediment and onion dome.

Armagh, Co Armagh

The study of church towers and steeples would occupy another book, so this rather untypical one must suffice.

Ormeau Avenue, Belfast

A late Victorian mock-mediaeval fountain imitating 14th century Eleanor Crosses, covered in carving and texts.

Belmont Road, Belfast

This distinctive timber tower is the crowning glory of a Victorian school building.

Donegall Square, Belfast

One of the side-shows of Belfast's Wrenaissance City Hall, whose main dome dominates Royal Avenue.

177

Derry, Co L'derry

Lurgan, Co Armagh

Bangor, Co Down

Victorian turrets and roofs often terminate in wrought-iron crestings like these. Note the rainwater downpipe straggling down one side of the Derry tower. The Lurgan cresting is lopsided, suggesting it may have incorporated a weathercock at one time.

A garden wall rather than a building, this obelisk is partly a folly and partly a boundary marker.

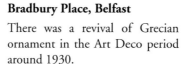

Armagh, Co Armagh

Bradbury Place, Belfast

Bangor, Co Down

Urns were a popular ornament on 18th century buildings, such as this terrace of about 1770.

There was a revival of Grecian ornament in the Art Deco period around 1930.

This otherwise Classical portico carries a weathercock with the vane to pick up the wind shaped rather like a flag.

Benburb, Co Tyrone

Set atop some rather fancy leadwork this is the archetypal weathercock, with an arrow for the windvane.

Portrush, Co Antrim

A conjunction of two finials, one being a weathercock with flag vane, the other with sprouts of metallic flowers.

Glenarm, Co Antrim

A fish weathercock swimming atop the Italianate former courthouse of the seaside village.

Fivemiletown, Co Tyrone

Appropriately for a railway station, this weathercock takes the form of a locomotive.

Bradbury Place, Belfast

A copper galleon in full sail as the weathercock on a charming gazebo erected in the 1930s.

Sandhurst Road, Belfast

A musician's weathercock, with a unique electric guitar weathervane and heraldically-painted frills.

Bargeboards

At first sight, bargeboards appear to be another of those vestigial appendices that have outlived whatever usefulness they may originally have had. In fact most people couldn't actually say what a bargeboard is.

Of course like most traditional details they were put there for a purpose. They are usually set a few inches out from the gable and carry the slates out sufficiently far to prevent rain from dripping off the roof down the gable. They also protect the ends of the slating battens from rot.

Their decorative function is obvious, as deep eaves give the roof a visual strength, and the shadows cast by a decorative bargeboard greatly enliven an elevation. Finally, the sheer variety of patterns and the opportunity they provide for adding bright colours up at roof level make bargeboards one of the most lively of traditional details.

This section also looks at eaves details, both carved eaves boards that often echo bargeboards and corbels that support gutters.

Downpatrick, Co Down

Sadly we rarely see bargeboards up close because they are fitted at roof level, their facets and intricacies often seen just as a flash of colour.

Newcastle, Co Down **Castlerock, Co L'derry** **Castlerock, Co L'derry**

In its simplest form, the bargeboard is a plain board (sometimes known as a fascia board) running in line with the roof joists and set a few inches proud of the gable, where it can protect the ends of the slating battens. With a little thought it can be converted to a bargeboard by carving a comma at the end (*left*) or cutting the lower edge to a wavy line (*centre and right*).

Tennant Street, Belfast **Comber, Co Down** **Ballywalter, Co Down**

The unusual example from about 1910 uses fretted carving below a mansard roof.

Instead of a wavy line the lower edge can be notched (*centre*) or made into a line of teeth (*right*) to catch the eye and ready to create interesting shadows when the sun comes out.

Rostrevor, Co Down

A formal and intrictate fretwork pattern providing a neat geometrical trim to a gable.

Coleraine, Co L'derry

A steeply-pitched gable with fretted flower pattern, and a small ridge finial at the crest.

Rosetta Avenue, Belfast

When picked out with a light colour even very simple fretted patterns can create effective eaves details.

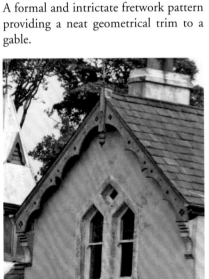

Greyabbey, Co Down

A simple and heavy bargeboard giving an ancient appearance. Unusually, the ends are supported on corbels.

Antrim, Co Antrim

For this bargeboard the fretted pattern underlines a wavy pattern broken up with small circles and the cartwheel pattern at the base of the fascia. The depth of the eaves creates a sort of peaked cap over the windows.

Newcastle Co Down

A close look at the bottom of a simple bargeboard with incised decoration, over ornamental brickwork.

Bangor, Co Down

A picturesque effect is obtained in this terrace by the alternation of gables and dormers, both carrying the same paper-doily pattern of bargeboard over their round-headed windows.

Sion Mills, Co Tyrone

A bargeboard with pierced base and chamfered board. There is an additional moulding supporting the slates.

Glenarm, Co Antrim

A boldly-toothed bargeboard on deep eaves with a highly contrasting paint scheme.

Crawfordsburn, Co Down

A chocolate box confection with an openly carved bargeboard on wide deep eaves.

Hilden, Co Antrim

A freely winding ribbon bargeboard. Although the building is mainly stone there is brick on the chimney line.

Donegall Pass, Belfast

The paint scheme here underlines the distinction between the fascia and finial and the ribbon fretwork.

Castlerock, Co L'derry

Situated on the north coast beside the sea and gulls, this white bargeboard is highly evocative of breaking waves, their crests emphasised by the trim edging of the boards.

Portglenone, Co Antrim

A simple wavy bargeboard with a neat matching crossbar at the top of the gable.

Rosslea, Co Fermanagh

This bargeboard looks like a sequence of teardrops, the appearance enhanced by the recesses in each drop.

Warrenpoint, Co Down

An unusual effect with a bay window slated in under the gable bargeboard like a curly wig.

Markethill, Co Armagh

Possibly a unique bargeboard, which somehow looks to have been fitted upside down.

Albertbridge Road, Belfast

A lively bargeboard with fretted teardrops, an intricately wavy board, and tall finial.

Lindsayville, Co Tyrone

Magnificently deep eaves set off by a scalloped bargeboard. The staining on the gable is tar from the chimney.

Dunmurry, Co Antrim

The same detail with alternating notches and rings is used at different scales on the gable and porch bargeboards.

Coleraine, Co L'derry

A scalloped bargeboard with the spandrels carved out for lightness, and a drop finial.

Coleraine, Co L'derry

A strange mixture of loops at each end of the bargeboard and vertical pendants in the middle.

Coleraine, Co L'derry

Also in Coleraine, and possibly by the same joiner, these pendants end in arrow heads.

Rostrevor, Co Down

A bold scalloped bargeboard with the scoops separated by uncompromising arrows.

Dungannon, Co Tyrone

A very delicate scalloped bargeboard with an onion knob ornament between each wave.

187

Caledon, Co Tyrone **Caledon, Co Tyrone** **Boardmills, Co Down**

A common motif on bargeboards (and elsewhere) is the fleur-de-lis, a stylised lily that looks rather like a spear-head. It is nomally used perpendicular to its base (*left and right*), but is sometimes (*centre*) found perpendicular to the ground instead. The Boardmills example shows a neat solution to the finial junction.

Holywood, Co Down

Trailing shamrocks and diamonds grace this gable, while on the ridge is a complementary cresting of fleur-de-lis and crosses. The plain rendered walls can be greatly enlivened by the painted bargeboards.

Boardmills, Co Down

A more abstract trailing bargeboard, incorporating circles and lilies that cast an intricate shadow.

Armagh, Co Armagh

A bold but unusually flat bargeboard, dated 1857. Such a bargeboard might be eighteen inches deep.

Derry, Co L'derry

A mid-Victorian bargeboard with a pattern made up from scrolls and diamonds.

Bessbrook, Co Armagh

Early Victorian bargeboards were often heavily carved using substantial timbers, and the mill village of Bessbrook has a number of bargeboards like this on communal buildings such as this schoolhouse.

189

Groomsport, Co Down

Once a joiner has mastered simple waves and scallops he can set his sights on lacier fancies such as this of about 1880.

Upperlands, Co L'derry

A well-contained creeper is carved into this bargeboard, with all its leaves turned into the curves of the main branch.

Cushendall, Co Antrim

This bargeboard incorporates a Celtic knot pattern, and there are leaves carved on the side of the porch.

Newtownards, Co Down

An intricately carved apex board with impressive finial and large cartwheel terminations. This is a strange building with part of the roof (*on the right*) castellated.

Woodstock Road, Belfast

Tendrils of ivy are packed into this bargeboard and the carved triangle of the apex board behind the finial. The gable has heavily rusticated stuccowork.

Randalstown, Co Antrim

Although Victorian in date, this bargeboard was based on a mediaeval pattern that had been published.

Strangford, Co Down

The thickness of the bargeboard timber allows for the fretwork to be given chamfered edges that catch the light.

Ballyclare, Co Antrim

A bargeboard in context - elaborate as they often are bargeboards can be matched by ornament elsewhere.

Comber, Co Down

A dignified fascia supported on carved brackets. Note the lantern in its iron supports over the gateway.

Whiteabbey, Co Antrim

Brackets support a deep eaves, which is decorated only by the skeleton apex framework.

Cookstown, Co Tyrone

The paired joists appear to be supporting the roof but are probably just decorative, with their faceted ends.

Portglenone, Co Antrim

A plain bargeboard ornamented rather severely with some faceted rectangles and a discreet kneeler.

Lisburn Road, Belfast

An intricately carved park gate lodge with an unusual bargeboard ornamented with sunflower heads and faceted rectangles. In imitation of mediaeval houses, the gable is jettied out and the window is an oriel.

Newcastle, Co Down

With no attempt to carve the main fascia board, the moulding above it is notched, and there is a further moulding over it.

Randalstown, Co Antrim

A rather over the top bargeboard at a gamekeeper's lodge, with massive carvings and several layers of mouldings set on a deep eaves.

Sion Mills, Co Tyrone

The simplicity of the finial, cross-piece and spandrel on the gable is made up for by the intricacy of the ironwork at the apex.

Lisburn, Co Antrim

A handsome and very definite gable design, with scrolled foliage symmetrically placed inside the apex board. The plain terracotta finial is part of the ridge as there is no true timber finial.

Brookeborough, Co Fermanagh

An apex board supported on small kneelers and filled with a pair of very simple shamrocks.

Newcastle, Co Down

A neat apex board supported on kneelers is set above a bay window. (*Compare* p.186).

University Street, Belfast

Ten years can make a big difference to architectural details. Most of the original bargeboard, eaves and corner windows (*above*) have survived unaltered, but for some reason the entire apex board has been replaced (*below*).

Armagh, Co Armagh

A comparatively modern building with half-timbered gable and shallow bow window, probably about 1930.

Blackwatertown, Co Tyrone

Dated 1843, this quirky gate lodge has an intricately carved bargeboard with fan-shaped geometric decoration and mottoes (including the name John Lawson and "Good Speed").

Caledon, Co Tyrone

Another lettered bargeboard, after the manner of mediaeval stonework which often carried dates and monograms.

Castlerock, Co L'derry

A frilly deep eaves board for the BNCR railway platforms, decorated with acroteria both ways up.

Rathcoole Street, Belfast

The ribbon-patterned bargeboard is echoed in an eaves board of the same pattern below the gutter.

Armagh, Co Armagh

A combination of decorative brackets and a picket design eaves board making a very rich support for the gutter.

Coalisland, Co Tyrone

A strange eaves decoration that is too shallow to be kneelers and too big to be dentils.

Carnlough, Co Antrim

A subtle fluted stucco decoration on the eaves of this straightforward building, allowing the architraves full value.

Castlereagh Street, Belfast

Sadly on its last legs, this was obviously a very intricate eaves at one time, with frieze, dentils and iron parapet.

Palestine Street, Belfast

Brick "specials" were made for use at the eaves of houses, either as corbels or as dogtooth ornament.

Derry, Co L'derry

The spacing of these brackets above the string course makes them look almost like toytown decoration.

Warrenpoint, Co Down

Obviously neither the little brackets nor the scrolled corbels at the window are functional.

Castlereagh Street, Belfast

An elegant cornice created from the frequent slender curved brackets under the deep eaves.

Derry, Co L'derry

Heavy pairs of double brackets support this eaves, making a strong feature of the fascia line. The painted lettering below is well matched to the style of the building which probaby dates from about 1900.

Newry, Co Down

At first sight just another set of paired eaves corbels, until you notice the detailed ornament on them, and then the grotesque heads between each pair of brackets, wearing turbans and helmets.

Rathgar Street, Belfast

The painted scooped cornice picks up the painted porches and the striped polychrome brickwork.

197

Cliftonville Road, Belfast

A terrace of early 19th century houses with an eaves detail derived from Greek temples.

Malone Road, Belfast

A late Victorian terrace with close-packed corbels supporting a deep gutter. The elevation is dominated by the full-height round bow windows and their turreted gable roofs, the interest of the building being mostly at roof level.

Castle Place, Belfast

A complex eaves detail from the mid-19th century, embracing dentils and a vegetable frieze.

Great Victoria Street, Belfast

Great Victoria Street, Belfast

College Gardens, Belfast

Many Victorian buildings have ogee gutters - with the moulded front and flat bottom seen above, supported on brackets or corbels. There was often a frieze *(left)* between the corbels, and sometimes *(right)* drip mouldings.

In this case the brackets have become dentils underneath the eaves, while the cornice consists of faceted rectangles.

Florenceville Avenue, Belfast

Newmills, Co Tyrone

Taking every opportunity for decoration, this mid-Victorian house even has frills on the gutters.

It was possible to have additional ornaments cast onto gutters when they were being manufactured, hence the acroteria cast onto this gutter *(left)*, while its downpipes *(right)* are panelled and held by cross-shaped holderbats.

Dungannon, Co Tyrone

While ogee gutters were often supported on a corbel course, half round gutters needed iron brackets to support them. Scotch brackets would be neatly driven into the wall or fixed to joists; however these examples are boastfully ornamental.

Donegall Street, Belfast

Templepatrick, Co Antrim

When rainwater has to be collected from more than one source or through a wall it is collected in a rainwater hopper.

Coleraine, Co L'derry

This imaginative concoction is an all-in-one hopper and gargoyle, gathering water without ejecting it into the street.

Comber, Co Down

A simple design of about 1920, incorporating the heart shape so beloved of Arts & Crafts designers.

North Street, Belfast

Dates were often incorporated in rainwater hoppers, even as late as 1928. Note the exterior alarm bell.

Limavady, Co L'derry

Georgian buildings generally liked to hide their gutters in lead valleys behind a parapet, gathered and discharged into internal downpipes so that the eye wasn't distracted from the symmetry of the elevations by functional pipework.

Enniskillen, Co Fermanagh

The public side of a parapet might be balustraded or panelled and ornamented with wreaths or sculpture.

Bangor, Co Down

A late 19th century parapet, supported on brackets and terminating in a sort of pedimented pilaster.

Bangor, Co Down

A splendid piece of stuccowork, with the balustrade broken by a dated pediment and terminated by urns at each end; dentils supporting the cornice and the spandrels between the arches covered in plant decoration.

Walls

Of all elements, it is perhaps walls that show the most distinctive character as we move from county to county in Ulster. Not only does each county have a distinctive geology that dictates the building materials used in walls, but there are the cultural differences - English, Scots, Irish, Italian - which dictate how those materials are used in different ways.

Brick was almost universally being used by the end of the 19th century but even it varies from area to area, with different clays being used and bricks being baked in different ways. Many Ulster buildings are rendered in an attempt to weatherproof them or make them look grander than they actually were.

Whether the walls are stone or simple mud, they dictate the shape of buildings, and when painted are a most important element in giving a building character. Painting can also be used to define boundaries, whether locally by quoinstones or more widely by painting gables or boundary walls.

Annahilt, Co Down

Snails are often found sheltering in damp locations on stone boundary walls, enjoying the lime on which their shells are, ultimately, built.

Kenbane Head, Co Antrim

Our oldest surviving structures are stone buildings, like this 16th century castle built of local basalt rubble stone.

Narrow Water, Co Down

This more sophisticated castle uses large stones (quoinstones) for strength at the corners and over openings.

Comber, Co Down

Probably 18th century work, this is Scrabo sandstone rubble laid to broken courses.

Glenarm, Co Antrim

Geologically Antrim comprises volcanic basalt laid over layers of chalk, here used with soldier heads over openings.

Annalong, Co Down

The Mourne Mountains are the source of local granite as used here, built in coursed rubble work.

Comber, Co Down

For ease and speed of construction, corners and openings in stone buildings were often built in brick.

Comber, Co Down

Roughly squared sandstone blocks are alternated with snecking stones packed in to take up irregularities.

Gracehill, Co Antrim

In some areas the mortar joints between stones are decorated with pebbles, a technique known as galleting. Apart from looking pleasant, the gallet stones would have helped to cover wide joints and to reduce the whiteness of new lime.

Enniskillen, Co Fermanagh

Limestone is found in Tyrone and Fermanagh. Here it is laid in finely-jointed ashlar construction.

Armagh, Co Armagh

The local stone around Armagh is a reddish conglomerate known as "Armagh marble" because it can take on a polish not unlike traditional marbles. It looks soft, but is actually quite a tough stone.

Bellaghy, Co Tyrone

Bricks were introduced to Ulster in the 17th century, when this wall was built nearly six feet thick.

Limavady, Co L'derry

Early bricks were made by hand, and show clearly the moulding of the clay and irregularity of the fired bricks.

Armagh, Co Armagh

Georgian brick buildings were generally built in Flemish bond, that is with alternating headers and stretchers as here. In this case the short ends (headers) appear to have been fired differently from the long sides, making a pattern.

Annadale Avenue, Belfast

By the end of the 19th century there were many local brickworks, the Annadale works making many specials.

Pakenham Street, Belfast

Although Belfast's basic brick was a cheerful orange-red, other bricks were mixed in to add patterns.

Euterpe Street, Belfast

In later or cheaper construction, English garden wall bond became the norm (three courses of headers followed by one of stretchers). Use of differently coloured bricks around openings had become the norm by the 1880s.

207

Alfred Street, Belfast

Following the publication of John Ruskin's *Stones of Venice* in the 1850s, flat tracery windows like this became fashionable, and were often ornamented in Venetian Gothic style by adding tiles, stone and differently coloured bricks.

Maryville Street, Belfast

Once one of the longest streets of brick housing in the city, Maryville had taller houses with this Greek key pattern.

Maymont Street, Belfast

The effect of polychrome bricks and subtly different paint colours along a street can be delightful.

Donegall Pass, Belfast

The ingenuity that went into different patterns of polychrome brickwork was amazing. Here there are panels of tumbled cream brickwork below the eaves as well as the more common brick corbels and string courses.

Lurgan, Co Armagh

As well as ordinary bricks, terracotta panels and vents were made by some brickworks.

Eglantine Avenue, Belfast *(top)*; **Antrim Co Antrim** *(left)*; **Union St, Belfast** *(rt)*

Antrim, Co Antrim *(top)*;
Donegall Avenue, Belfast *(bottom)*

Terracotta vents let air into rooms and timber sub-floors.

The Mount, Belfast *(upper left)*; **Antrim, Co Antrim** *(upper right)*;
Cushendall, Co Antrim *(lower left)*; **North Street, Belfast** *(lower right)*.

The Cushendall vent uses a Celtic knot; the North Street date is boldly Art Nouveau in style. The others refer to Renaissance models from book printing.

Royal Avenue, Belfast

Terracotta could be used to construct an entire façade, using standardised components in Gothic or Classical styles, available from extensive catalogues. This building uses brick near the top, but much of it is terracotta (*right*).

Newry, Co Down

Unglazed terracotta is orange-red, but a glazed version called faience comes in various colours.

Castle Place, Belfast

In this Art Nouveau faience building the standard catalogue items were supplemented with individually designed wrought ironwork. The original windows had a matching complexity.

Downpatrick, Co Down

Because they were readily washed down, terracotta and glazed tiles were popular in grocers' and butchers' shops like this. The detail here is more Classical.

Warrenpoint, Co Down

Occasionally buildings are found with an exposed elevation clad in slate to prevent water penetration.

Bellarena, Co L'derry

Tiles were often incorporated into late Victorian façades as a decorative feature. Here it is functional as well, giving the name of a railway station in the nicely varied warm tones of old tiles.

Bangor, Co Down

Quarry tiles are often found on house paths and in hallways, usually laid diagonally or in geometric patterns. Here they are also used for the dados in the halls of a pair of houses.

Dublin Road, Belfast

Tiles were particularly popular in pubs, the Crown Bar being the best-known example.

Teemore, Co Fermanagh

Yes, cottages really can be built in mud, usually gathered from the nearby fields and built up in mass (*see below*), often creating soft curving walls that match the shape of the thatch overhead.

Teemore, Co Fermanagh

Part of the same cottage has been built or patched in turfs set in lime mortar, which is unusual.

Dungannon, Co Tyrone

Unfortunately mud cottages are very fragile and can be lost rapidly if the roof fails and water gets at the clay.

Annalong, Co Down

When the thatch begins to go and a thatcher isn't available or affordable, sheets of corrugated iron ("tin") are often put on instead, and occasionally whole buildings clad in tin are found.

Newtownbutler, Co Fermanagh

Whether built of stone, brick or mud, many early buildings were rendered (plastered) with a coat of lime and grit.

Donaghadee, Co Down

For all the antiquity of Grace Neill's pub, the rendering looks suspiciously lumpy and overdone.

Saintfield, Co Down

By the 18th century many buildings were being rendered with smooth lime plaster lined to represent stonework.

Armagh. Co Armagh

When plasterers began to imitate carvings and other mouldings they were working with stucco.

Lurgan, Co Armagh

Not content with simple lining, plasterers started imitating vermiculated stone and other finishes.

Waringstown, Co Down

In the 1920s this plastering technique was the way to achieve ye instant olde-worlde effect.

Comber, Co Down

In this terrace of rendered houses the plaster is formed into a running string course of eyebrows over the windows.

Ballyclare, Co Antrim

An abrupt change of pitch for the plaster string courses as this terrace negotiates a hill.

Portglenone, Co Antrim

The winding plaster string course here creates ornamental panels between the windows.

Ballyclare, Co Antrim

In the early 20th century a combination of roughcast walls with smooth plaster decoration was common.

Aughnacloy, Co Tyrone

Sometimes pebbles or glass were set into the fresh render on some panels for added effect.

Bangor, Co Down

Another common technique in the 1930s was exposing some bricks or tiles amongst the render.

Newcastle, Co Down

Limestone pebbles are set into wet plaster between the stucco features on this seaside house.

Strangford, Co Down

Rather casually placed scallop shells and coloured glass decorate a house overlooking the shore.

Markethill, Co Armagh

A panel of broken coloured glass provides some light relief in an otherwise more formal elevation.

Ballyshannon, Co Donegal

Some serious pebble sticking went on at this house, using broken crockery and glass as well as limpets (*right*) to create a series of intersecting squares and rectangles that can only be seen from quite close to.

Downpatrick, Co Down

This bizarre effect (which has no masonry equivalent) seems to have used the top and bottom of a wine bottle.

Downhill, Co L'derry

If you were an archbishop or a bank you would of course use stone for your columns and pilasters. Labour was comparatively cheap and stone readily available.

Waring Street, Belfast

In 1820 the Belfast merchants built their meeting-place using granite, not the most easily worked stone but famously durable.

May Street, Belfast

A handsome Ionic capital (supposed to have been based by the Greeks on a ram's horns) on a music hall.

Lower Crescent, Belfast

Corinthian capitals combine the ram's horns with acanthus leaves to form a complex sculpture.

Magherafelt, Co L'derry

A free-form capital devised by architects in the Art Nouveau style about 1910, loosely derived from the Ionic.

Drumbeg, Co Antrim

When the main building material is small rubble, large corner stones are required to stabilise the wall.

Ballycastle, Co Antrim

When translated into plaster, quoinstones have no function other than to demarcate property boundaries.

Glenarm, Co Antrim

When stone is carved with a texture like this it is described as "vermiculated" (worm-eaten).

Carn, Co Armagh (*above*);
Portglenone, Co Antrim (*below*)

A crude attempt at vermiculation (*above*) and a more sophisticated one (*below*).

Dundrum, Co Down

A neat interpretation of vermiculation, outlined with a black line as would be impossible in plain stone.

Upper Crescent, Belfast

An accomplished terrace of neo-Classical buildings, this terrace has channelled ground floors and vermiculated quoins.

Comber, Co Down; Comber, Co Down; Kilkeel, Co Down; Portaferry, Co Down

Sometimes buildings are delineated by having pilasters (flattened columns) at either side of the front elevation, as with the two Comber examples here. In the Kilkeel example the quoins are like a stack of dominoes. In the Portaferry example (*right*) only every other quoin is present, which was considered stylish in the 1930s.

Belcoo, Co Fermanagh; Belcoo, Co Fermanagh; Dundrum, Co Down; Ballynahinch, Co Down

The Belcoo quoinstones are very idiosyncratic and obviously by the same plasterer; the brown one (*second from left*) incorporates a date of 1944. The Dundrum example (*second from right*) starts out as a charmingly naive fluted pilaster, then gives up and carries on as ordinary quoins. At Ballynahinch (*right*) the quoins are alternately pennant-shaped.

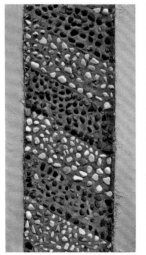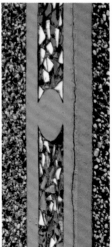

Ballygawley, Co Tyrone; Charlemont, Co Armagh; Edentrillick, Co Down

Some home-made quoins: neatly laid-out mussel-shells at Ballygawley (*left*); black and white pebbles as are common round Charlemont (*centre*); and at Edentrillick (*right*) the pilaster is panelled out in broken glass and pebbles.

Kircubbin, Co Down

It is not uncommon for quoins to start off in one form and end up quite differently in the next storey.

Dundrum, Co Down

A glorious concatenation of quoins, pebbles and vermiculation as two ambitious properties run side by side.

Glenarm, Co Antrim

This stack of quoins seems to break every rule, not being on a corner nor quite at a boundary, and highly unstable.

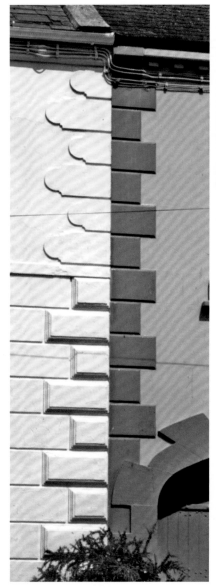

Coalisland, Co Tyrone

A neat solution to fitting quoinstones on a chamfered corner (with rising ground dealt with by the plinth).

Castlewellan, Co Down

If your plasterer isn't keen on three-dimensional work but your painter is, you can get this kind of quoin.

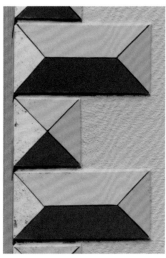

Killyleagh, Co Down

Ambitious fielded quoins and pennant quoins on the left, no-nonsense quoins from his neighbour on the right.

Castlewellan, Co Down

The secret is to have four similar colours so that light appears to come from one side as well as above.

Ballykeel Loan Ends, Co Down

One of the most subtle and convincing of painted quoins, with the window drawing the eye away.

Markethill, Co Armagh

Before the advent of modern paints, every house in Ireland was spruced up annually with a coat of whitewash. Over the years the lime built up a finish that was both protective and beautiful.

Annahilt, Co Down

Strong primary colours could be applied to the windows and to the railings alike and often work well with limewash.

Ballydugan, Co Down

Sometimes earth colours were added to limewash to give strong ochres or pinks. As the colours were never quite the same from year to year a rich patina of shades developed.

Glynn, Co Antrim

Perhaps because of our grey climate, bright (or even clashing) colours have often been used. Note here the window reveals are picked out in red to set off the white sashes.

Glenarm, Co Antrim

There are few rules - you can paint window surrounds, plinths and doors in one colour and sashes in another, or just pick them out in a contrasting colour from the walls. If possible at least two of the colours should match the dog.

Comber, Co Down

Walls are usually lighter than doors and windows - yet the very boldness of this scheme seems to work.

Enniskillen, Co Fermanagh

Pink is a very personal choice, but the forthright contrast of wall and window surrounds here works well.

Downpatrick, Co Down

Generally speaking the walls and chimneys should be of the same colour, but perhaps not if they are yellow.

Downpatrick, Co Down

This strong blue would be too much on a bigger building, but on a modest house it is a welcome spot of colour.

Donegall Road, Belfast

In the "wee palaces" that made up much of inner-city Belfast doorsteps were scrubbed and brick annually painted.

Cullybackey, Co Antrim

There is a tradition in Co Antrim of painting basalt stone (which is nearly black) black, and lime mortar (which is nearly white) white to make the effect more workmanlike. The colour of brick is a matter of choice.

Palmer Street, Belfast

On the same principle as the Cullybackey example, you could paint reddish brick red and whitish brick white.

223

Lurgan, Co Armagh

Although a simple terrace of tightly-packed red brick houses, the effect of the differently coloured window reveals makes for a warm and lively streetscape.

Bangor, Co Down

In this terrace the wall colours are varied from house to house and the brightly-painted bargeboards and bristling chimney stacks draw the eye up to roof level.

Carnlough, Co Antrim

In a rather drab rendered terrace the window surrounds painted blue, pink and yellow give the individual houses identity.

Ballyhalbert, Co Down

These single-storey fishermen's cottages are beautifully painted with subtle shades of white, yellow and pink with stronger colours on windows or reveals.

Ballyhalbert, Co Down

A cut above your average paint scheme, this seems to have taken inspiration from Continental sgraffiti decoration.

Articlave, Co L'derry

How to make a standard Housing Trust porch stand out from the crowd, as long as you don't mind the sightseers. For a few glorious years every house in this estate vied to be the most gaudy and decorated, until someone lost their nerve.

Armagh, Co Armagh

Perhaps inspired by those large liquorice allsorts, this was at the same time an advertisement and an editorial.

Groomsport, Co Down

Walls and roofs define the shape of a building. A typical Ulster house looks something like this, two stories high with windows in the front and back walls, chimneys on the gable walls, the roof parallel to the front, and a central door.

Kilwaughter, Co Antrim

Cottages traditionally extended lengthwise and sometimes upwards, as need and opportunity presented themselves.

Downpatrick, Co Down

Changes in level and tight sites often inspire interesting solutions that would not have been arrived at simply by planning a building on the drawing board. They can also grow organically over time with changes of ownership or purpose.

Donaghadee, Co Down

Exceptions to the norm are always interesting, like this powder store built for blasting out the local harbour.

Cushendall, Co Antrim

The five-storey curfew tower and dungeon in Cushendall is a folly but also the focal point of the town.

Dungannon, Co Tyrone

Sometimes an industry will create curious structures, such as this castellated gateway to the Dungannon reservoir.

Ormeau Road, Belfast

Sometimes industrial processes require extraodinary structures like hoppers and gasoliers.

Carnlough, Co Antrim

When industries close or go into decline their old buildings can be adapted for new uses, as this former corn mill was adapted into a butcher's shop.

Bangor, Co Down

Often the shape comes about simply from the circumstances of the site, as in this corner building which follows a gentle curve linking two streets.

Bangor, Co Down

Two more rendered corner buildings, the first a gently-softened corner with considerable dignity, the second an acutely-angled corner emphasised by a pediment that has the impetus of a ship's prow.

Bangor, Co Down

Unfortunately, curved or chamfered walls are hard to roof, hence the abrupt change of plan at this roof.

Fivemiletown, Co Tyrone

Another unusual solution to the problem of matching corner and roof, with a cantilevered gutter.

Lagan Street, Belfast

More often the cantilever occurs on the ground floor, and is particularly popular for pubs.

Cushendall, Co Antrim

An elegant resolution of corner and roof, with the answer picked out in the paint scheme.

Moy, Co Tyrone

Perhaps less elegant, but undoubtedly useful as a place to stand and watch the world go by.

Belleek, Co Fermanagh

In the traditional and vernacular world, most details arise out of a compromise between utility and ambition. Nowadays a building is too often either just utilitarian or like the stage set from an American soap opera.

Great Victoria Street, Belfast

A lesson not just in how to turn an awkward corner with a building, but how to make a whole eyesore of a building into something that lifted the spirits as it set sail in an urban car park. The muralist was Naomi McBride, turning the Royal Naval Association's building, flues, oil tanks and all, into an inner-city merchant ship.

Linfield Industrial Estate, Belfast

The once-ubiquitous King Billy murals have been superseded by many more aggressive ones in the last forty years.

Rockview Street, Belfast

A very glossy and freshly-painted mural ready to be scorched again by the annual bonfire.

Bangor, Co Down

A recently imported political activist making a point between the windows of a pub.

Sevastopol Street, Belfast

Books have been written about the Ulster murals, representing both persuasions, and they have become quite a tourist attraction, which is not what they set out to be. The muralists have become very proficient and their work almost Establishment.

Sevastopol Street, Belfast

Belfast humour tends not to take things seriously however, and some murals have attracted unofficial comment.

Mourne Mountains, Co Down

The typical field pattern in Ulster is small in scale, with walls often running in parallel up the side of a mountain; here the fields are more irregular and follow the contours of the land, to keep sheep in rather than grow crops.

Mourne Mountains, Co Down

The pattern of drystone walling varies from county to county and is a study in itself. This is built from granite erratics.

Portadown, Co Armagh

A rather sophisticated stile over a church wall. More often there is a kissing gate or other simpler opening.

Annalong, Co Down

Mourne granite is hard to cut and shape but some estate walls were built in neatly cut stone like this.

Donaghadee, Co Down

The soft red sandstone coping on this sea wall has been savagely eroded by decades of storm breakers.

Gates & Ironwork

After timber, iron is perhaps the most versatile material used in traditional construction. It is used in gates and railings of course, but also in pumps, lamps, garden seats, conservatories and fountains.

The simplest form of iron was wrought iron, at one time used by blacksmiths to make horseshoes, tools and railings. Mass-produced cast iron patterns became common in the early 19th century and made more intricate designs possible at affordable prices. At the end of the 19th century steel became common and it became the standard metal in building.

Wrought iron is malleable and lends itself to unique designs, but is now hard to get; cast iron is brittle; and steel is strong but liable to rust very quickly. Each has *les défauts de ses qualités*.

During World War II metal railings and gates were collected as part of the war effort to create munitions. Unfortunately the authors of the plan had failed to realise that cast iron cannot just be melted down and converted into steel, and sadly most of the ornamental railings that had been collected were just dumped at sea.

Camden Street, Belfast

Often railings consist of a number of castings combined with steel or wrought iron. In this case the umbrella head was a separate casting from the trunk linking it to the top rail.

233

Lisburn, Co Antrim

Perhaps the simplest form of railing is a succession of hooped uprights, often used in municipal parks because it has no spikes for children to impale themselves on, although they can probably jam their heads between the uprights if they try.

Ormeau Embankment, Belfast

Hooped railings in front of a row of mid-19th century cottages provide privacy as well as protection.

Seaforde, Co Down

For the private owner who doesn't mind every other intruder getting speared this is a mixture of hoop and spike.

Castleward, Co Down

Plain spear-head railings from about 1830, with bosses hammered in below the heads and at the base.

Lisburn, Co Antrim

Substantial spear-head railings with heavy top rails and uprights. Often modern railings are too light.

Glenanne, Co Armagh

The beauty of wrought ironwork lies in its subtle irregularities since it is hand-made, and the quirky whorls on this gate are an excellent example, none of them quite the same but all are attempts to make the same thing.

Moy, Co Tyrone

Sometimes additional railings are required to fill a gap or change of level and this quadrant of railings results.

Hillsborough, Co Down

High quality 18th century wrought-iron gates relocated at Hillsborough from Richhill.

Dundrum, Co Down

An additional set of uprights is often inserted at lower level to deter dogs and very small children.

Hillsborough, Co Down

Modern wrought ironwork uses stand-ardised components and lack the variety of handmade work.

Mullen, Co Monaghan

Cast iron made possible heavy ornamental corner pillars for railings, which would have been impossible in wrought work.

Enniskillen, Co Fermanagh

In no time, the corner posts became a feature in themselves, though the blacksmith sometimes had to add to them.

Cliftonville Road, Belfast

A common arrangement in cast railings was to alternate uprights with double balustrades.

Cushendall, Co Antrim

Castings would carry intricate embossed decoration, evoking past styles of architecture.

Belleek, Co Fermanagh

Cast iron could even imitate nature herself, as in this mesh of vine leaves - obviously designed for inns.

College Square North, Belfast

The pineapple became a popular architectural ornament when it was introduced to Britain in the 1600s.

Caledon, Co Tyrone

The Roman fasces was a bundle of birch rods carried in procession, here used as cast-iron posts.

Toomebridge, Co Antrim

A couple of arms wrestling one another form railings round the eccentric John Cary tomb at Duneane.

Newbliss, Co Monaghan

A much calmer iron hand loosely acts as a hinge for a gatepost with an umbrella top.

Derry, Co L'derry

With cast-iron panels it became possible to forget about the regularity of uprights and to devise much more organic designs such as this on a flight of steps at a church, flanked by stone volutes at the sides.

Rostrevor, Co Down

An elegant diagonal trellis pattern in cast-iron panels set between posts and a handrail.

237

Armagh, Co Armagh

Although with some of the freedom of cast iron this looks to be locally fabricated.

Holywood, Co Down

Often cast-iron railings were made up of repeated panels with a mixture of uprights and freer patterns.

Moy, Co Tyrone

An interesting design that is based on a geometric trellis but also encompasses acroteria.

Rostrevor, Co Down

This pillar in a handrail is curiously decorated with a snail or ammonite and an umbrella top.

Stewartstown, Co Tyrone

Victorian handrails could be quite light and easy to grasp, but made up for their simplicity by interpolating elaborate supporting pillars, sometimes with twisted stems and leafy ornament as here.

Boardmills, Co Down

Since many Ulster houses were rural it made sense to use the same bar iron for house gates as for farm gates.

Moy, Co Tyrone

However, the blacksmith could be encouraged to apply his skills in extruding iron to the domestic gate.

Tullykin, Co Down

Wrought iron is malleable and easily formed but just as easy to deform, producing wonderful shapes.

Rosslea, Co Fermanagh

If the blacksmith was less talented he might get away with welding on a few standard spears.

Markethill, Co Armagh

In this simple gate the blacksmith's iron bosses at the junction of rails and bars make a strong statement.

Ballynahinch, Co Down

This hooped gate (with a row of spikes on top to deter flying dogs) has a nice sprung latch.

Ballynahinch, Co Down

Lisnagat, Co Armagh

The light ironwork gate with added scrolls, set between two handsome whitewashed pillars, with a box-lined path behind leading to the neatly colour-washed house, make a delightful scene.

Cushendall, Co Antrim

Two elaborate wrought-iron gates, the upper one with numerous tight scrolls, the lower with embossed leaves.

Ballydugan, Co Down

There are few latches that will fool a determined farm animal wanting to get out of a field, but this snake-headed latch might just deter the less determined one.

Donaghcloney, Co Down

Nearly as curly, this Art Nouveau shop gate probably dates from about 1910. Such a gate indicated that the shop was closed for business, but more kindly than a metal shutter.

High Street, Belfast

A large late Victorian metal gateway protecting an entrance in the centre of Belfast.

Castlewellan, Co Down

The head of a metal gateway had to include a suitable finial to the heavy central bars. This is dated 1894.

Lindsayville, Co Tyrone

Mr Henry's new gate incoporates a piece of bicycle engineering to commemorate his enthusiasm for cycling.

Markethill, Co Armagh

Although this simple pattern could have been made with wrought iron, cast iron enabled more complex mouldings.

Benburb, Co Tyrone

A formal gate given varied weight and texture by the casting process to produce a lively design.

Markethill, Co Armagh

Interesting cast-iron ornament including urn-shaped finials, with bosses filling the gap below the gate.

Crom, Co Fermanagh

Detail of cast-iron elements of an estate gate, much richer than would have been the case for a normal farm.

Portballintrae, Co Antrim   **Middletown, Co Armagh**

Two contrasting cast-iron gates, the first chunky with rather Gothic details (quatrefoils and traceried arches), the second quite delicate with varied free ornament and probably dating from about 1900.

Lisburn Road, Belfast

This shows how railings deal with a change of level at steps, and also how a gate can be fitted in discreetly.

Culrane, Co Antrim

Kissing gates - where a gate swings between two keepers, always being closed on one side if the other is open - are usually found at fields, but here used at a rural school to prevent children from rushing into the road.

Portadown, Co Armagh

The lych-gate is an English detail usually found in churches (the coffin could rest there before burial).

Gilford, Co Down

A canopied pedestrian entrance thoughtfully provided alongside the heavier vehicular entrance.

Armagh, Co Armagh

A gate that is no longer a gate, as it is easier to walk round it than go through it. Slimmers treat it as a challenge.

Ballywalter, Co Down

Although tubular steel is not an inspiring material, it doesn't have to be used just for five-barred gates, as this farmhouse entrance demonstrates, with its rising sun motif and scrollwork on top.

Donegall Pass, Belfast

There is a tradition of keeping horses and dogs in the Markets area of Belfast, and there is obviously a kennel here.

Newcastle, Co Down

A basic gate design decorated with the masons' set square and dividers and painted to match the porch behind.

Cranfield, Co Down

The combination of whitewashed gatepillars and bright red gate is a perfect example of how the agricultural landscape can enhance the natural landscape of gorse, thorn and mountains.

(*top row*) **Lindsayville, Co Tyrone; Mowhan, Co Armagh;** (*centre row*) **Kircubbin, Co Down; Newtownbutler, Co Fermanagh;** (*bottom row*) **Ballee, Co Down; Newtownbutler, Co Fermanagh**

Farm gates are often made from flat bars worked into variations on the five-barred gate theme, and traditionally set between stout round pillars (*centre left*). Where a gate leads to the house it is more likely to be divided and vertically barred.

Sion Mills, Co Tyrone

A piece of Old England transplanted into the west of Ulster, the linen village of Sion Mills was largely laid out by the English architect W F Unsworth using half timbering and other mediaeval detailing.

Hillsborough, Co Down

A simple wooden gate made special by the insertion of the shamrock motif cut out of the central panel.

Lisburn, Co Antrim

Perhaps a home-made gate, with the timber palisades shaped like a row of space rockets, or slender milk bottles.

Groomsport, Co Down

Fronting a holiday chalet, this gate with its ornamental capping was perhaps made or added to while away on wet weekends.

Killough, Co Down

An asymmetrical gate, the barred portion offering a glimpse to the garden beyond.

Castlerock, Co L'derry

A good example of the traditional Ulster gate pillars, built of local fieldstone, lightly harled and linked by a five-barred gate. Many have been lost when gates have been widened to accommodate modern farm machinery.

Dundrum, Co Down

An individual treatment of gate pillars, cleanly painted and decorated with coloured pebbles.

Brookeborough, Co Fermanagh

A pillar emerging through the morning mist topped with something that is a cross between an urn and a bird-bath.

Armagh, Co Armagh

The fine 18th century pillars moved from Armagh Palace to what Sir Charles Brett called "the archi-episcopal bungalow".

Castlerock, Co L'derry

A romanticised form of the traditional cylindrical pillar, capped with a witch's hat and a ball finial.

Lisburn Road, Belfast

Probably built about 1890, this pillar has a sandstone cube on top of a plinth of sandstone and limestone bands.

College Green, Belfast

Typically, substantial late Victorian houses had pillars of brick capped in sandstone. Note the leafy gate.

Rugby Road, Belfast

Although referring back to earlier models these tall pillars and urns were designed by Clough Williams-Ellis in 1936.

Antrim, Co Antrim

Cast iron was used for many late 19th century pillars, often in a skeletal form like this.

Lennoxvale, Belfast

Workmen taking the front off a cast-iron pillar, perhaps to repair its innards. Having discovered that it is empty, they are having to refer to the instruction manual before putting it back together again.

Ballynahinch and Newry, Co Down

The way cast iron could adopt an ecclesiastical style, such as the Perpendicular (*left*) made it popular for churches.

Stewartstown, Co Tyrone; Lurgan, Co Armagh

Solid iron pillars could achieve high strength with elegant lines.

Toomebridge, Co Antrim

With pillars shaped like ice cream cones and a gate that incorporates cats, ducklings, roses and a plethora of swans' heads, this was the entrance to Rarity Cottage, home of the local philanthropist, clergyman and alleged murderer John Cary.

Mowhan, Co Armagh

This stone set beside a gateway and about nine inches high, is said to be a mounting stone, for getting up on a horse.

Coleraine, Co L'derry

Downpatrick, Co Down

On many carriage entrances bollards were set up to protect the arrises from carelessly driven carts. These early ones were made of stone and blended in with the often cobbled streets.

Hill Street, Belfast

This unusual bollard is actually a ship's cannon half buried in the ground, muzzle upwards.

Skipper Street, Belfast

Sandy Row, Belfast

The classic carriageway bollard is cone-shaped like that on the *right*. Wheels might ride up the cone but would rapidly slide away again without damaging the wall. The foundry would often stamp its name beside the cone.

Ballycastle, Co Antrim

A bracketed lamp set over the entrance to a Georgian church. Lamps were put there to be seen as much as to see by.

Limavady, Co L'derry

A unique and very determined bollard with a baton clutched in its fist and a curved sloping base off which wheels would slide smoothly back to the ground. Hands were common ornaments in Victorian decoration and ornaments.

Hillsborough, Co Down

Before street lighting became standard, oil lamps were often set over railings in towns.

Greyabbey, Co Down

Window guards are put there to make cills uncomfortable for sitting on by persons or pigeons.

Oxford Street, Belfast

This guard follows the principle of the mediaeval caltrop, with a spike up in every direction.

Ballycastle, Co Antrim

A less vicious guard, with barley-sugar rails and leafy spandrels to the firmly-placed uprights.

Lurgan, Co Armagh

Like everything else about a building, guards need maintenance. Most are cast iron which rusts quite slowly, but are vulnerable at the points of contact with the wall and cill.

Saintfield, Co Down

An elegant and well-maintained guard, providing an element of privacy as well as ornamenting the street frontage. The date is probably late 19th century.

Armagh, Co Armagh

Armagh being a Classical city, it is appropriate that this guard uses the acroteria as its main theme, though the setting looks more recent.

Derry, Co L'derry

Victorian buildings, particularly commercial ones, could put ironwork on window cills at every level and sometimes along the gutter and cresting as well, to produce an effect of encrustation.

Armagh, Co Armagh   **Newry, Co Down**   **Warrenpoint, Co Down**

The large first-floor windows of Georgian buildings could sometimes be used as French windows thanks to the addition of iron balconies. These examples only serve individual windows, with ironwork similar to the patterns used in railings, and slatted iron floors to let the rain through.

(top and above) **Crawfordsburn, Co Down; Newcastle, Co Down**

The lower example has lovely free light ironwork and spandrels.

Carrickfergus, Co Antrim; Enniskillen, Co Fermanagh; Bangor, Co Down

When a balcony spans the full width of a house, or the perimeter of a bow window as with the Bangor example, it makes a very important statement on the front of the building but in quite an understated way.

(top and above) **Newcastle, Co Down**
(Right, top to bottom) **Bangor, Co Down; Albertbridge Road, Belfast; The Mount, Belfast**

The examples on the right all date from the end of the 19th century, the more delicate Newcastle examples probably slightly earlier.

Derry, Co L'derry

The iron porch of the former Carlisle Hotel, with cast-iron spandrels and cresting.

Berry Street, Belfast

The ornate porch of the National Club, with a harp in a bed of shamrock scrolls and tendrils.

Bangor, Co Down

A pair of cast-iron spandrels to balconies at the former Grand Hotel. The whole spandrel arch is decorated.

Holywood, Co Down

A cast-iron garden seat - perhaps not the most comfortable to sit on with its knobbly Gothic backrest and hard seat, but no doubt cushions were available.

Downhill Avenue, Belfast

Cast-iron ends for park benches - the seats would have been timber. A cherub is negotiating his way carefully through the foliage.

(clockwise from top left) **Newry, Co Down; Moy, Co Tyrone; Stewartstown, Co Tyrone; McMaster Street, Belfast; Lisburn, Co Antrim; Moy, Co Tyrone; Gracehill, Co Antrim**

With the exception of the roof cresting (*bottom right*) these are tie-bars, inserted into buildings to prevent walls from bowing out. The one at McMaster Street (*centre right*) was put in following World War II bombing in the area.

Bangor, Co Down

Every self-respecting Victorian castle had a clock tower and weathervane, visible from many parts of the estate.

Caledon, Co Tyrone

Most towns had a courthouse which served also as a market house and often had a cupola and clock tower.

Bangor, Co Down

This purpose-built clock tower was presented to the town by the Borough Rates Collector.

Newcastle, Co Down

It was the spread of the railways from the middle of the 19th century which made accurate timekeeping necessary.

Bessbrook, Co Armagh

As a model town, Bessbrook had to have a clock prominently available to its inhabitants.

Arthur Square, Belfast

It was always time to call in for a pint at Mooney's, as this clock reminded the passing tipplers.

Cookstown, Co Tyrone

This two-faced clock was built over a jeweller's shop, and the young man is consulting his pocket watch.

Fivemiletown, Co Tyrone

This clock marked the Petty Sessions of 1823, hence the crown and coat of arms.

Donegall Place, Belfast

Clocks were an excellent way to advertise your firm, and this was at Anderson & McAuley's department store.

Royal Avenue, Belfast

"The Tully" was cried by newspaper-sellers up and down the city after being printed in this building.

Royal Avenue, Belfast

The arrival of Art Deco led to clock faces becoming stylishly square, and fitting onto the building more easily.

Killyleagh & Gilford, Co Down

Two examples of inter-war clocks, the top one advertising a bank and the bottom one a chemist's shop.

Cushendall, Co Antrim

In early 19th century Cushendall the time was given out by the bell on the battlements of the Curfew Tower.

Ballymena, Co Antrim

The bell on the lodge of the People's Park was there to sound closing time before the park was locked up.

Hillsborough, Co Down

The old phone box, once ubiquitous but now replaced by mobiles and a number of less distinguished kiosks.

Bangor, Co Down

As there are so few horses around town these days, the old horse trough was filled with flowers. It was close to the market where animals would have gathered.

Bangor, Co Down

This U-boat gun was presented to the town by the Admiralty in 1919. To the frustration of generations of boys ever since, it seems to lack an adequate firing mechanism.

Enniskillen, Co Fermanagh

A Victorian wall letterbox still in daily use, with the crown and monogram above the slot.

Ballycastle, Co Antrim

An Edward VII pillar box. Despite several attempts in recent years, the classic box design has yet to be surpassed.

Mowhan, Co Armagh

In the days before mains water was widely available every farmyard had its pump, often something like this which would have drawn up clean water from nearby springs. Although these were very basic devices, the ironfounder would leave his name and trademark on them (*below*) in order to get repeat custom.

Derry, Co L'derry

If you've got it, flaunt it - a home-made letterbox for a firm of ironfounders. It is not known whether the design inspired customers to commission their own versions, but it fits well onto the building.

Aughnacloy, Co Tyrone

Belleek, Co Fermanagh

(above) **Markethill, Co Armagh**
*(below)***Helen's Bay, Co Down**

Larger pumps were placed in villages or near groups of houses as few had their own water supply, and many still remain as landmarks in the street. These wheel-driven pumps were particularly handsome.

This drinking fountain was placed on the railway station platform.

Ballygawley, Co Tyrone

Caledon, Co Tyrone

The rat-tail handled pumps (*see top right*) usually had a stand to place containers on (*see lower left*) and sometimes an iron plate behind recording the donation or decorated with mythological figures (*centre*).

Bangor, Co Down

A prefabricated iron fountain and memorial in the Moorish style.

Toomebridge, Co Antrim

John Cary strikes again. He obviously loved ironwork, for its durability and strength, its facility for making hands, and no doubt also for its ability to carry hectoring texts.

Newcastle. Co Down
Bangor, Co Down

Iron bandstands were once the pride of every seaside municipality.

263

Shops

Since one of the main reasons people congregate is to facilitate commerce, shops are one of the most common and typical building types in our towns and villages.

Early shops were little more than houses where goods were sold, but gradually they developed display windows and could be recognised as commercial units. As technology developed the windows became larger, glazing bars were dropped, and advertising developed from hanging out a picture of a teapot to sophisticated lettering with shadows and gilding.

Specialist shops began to appear and each developed distinctive appearances: pubs became gin palaces, more exotic and comfortable than the homes of their clients, chemists' shops acquired mysterious aromas and mystiques, and drapers decorated their shop windows with mannequins and swathes of fine cloths.

In the last few decades most shopfronts have degenerated to cheap plastic fascias and standardised logos, but there is little evidence to suggest that a traditional shopfront deters customers. In fact, you may find your mouth watering looking at some of the displays.

Lenaderg, Co Down

Until recently this little grocer's shop was still open under the direction of its nonagenarian proprietor. With the telephone kiosk outside and the confections within, this would have been the centre of village gossip.

265

Lindsayville, Co Tyrone

Many rural shops were farmhouses with a store of long-life provender under the stairs, but gradually they developed shelves and windows. This window is a recent enlargement.

Newtownards, Co Down

This seems likely to have been a shop, with the comparatively large window and the half-door, contrasting with the more typical panel door beside it.

Dungannon, Co Tyrone

A rudimentary shopfront, with a brick relieving arch visible above the lintel of the shop window, and no pediment. The paintwork extends beyond the pilasters over the brick quoins.

Saintfield, Co Down

This shopfront has the full entablature of a Victorian shop, but interestingly there are shutters to the front door. I like the tricky downpipe, too.

Ballynahinch, Co Down

A one-time shop that has reverted to being a residence, with a window display of hardy plants in cermaic jardinières. The folding outer doors of the porch were common in shops.

Armagh, Co Armagh

At one time there was a demand for temperance hotels, where a quiet night's sleep might be expected after the residents had retired with their Ovaltine.

Ballynahinch, Co Down

Once shops had become specialised rooms lined with shelves and storage, it became important to have a separate entrance for the family. Here there is a double door to the shop and a conventional door to the house.

Cushendall, Co Antrim

A handsome double-fronted shop with divided windows flanking the shop entrance, and a panel door to the left for the family.

Enniskillen, Co Fermanagh

Although the shop windows have been replaced, this retains its splendid (though almost capital-less) fluted columns supporting the long entablature.

Greyabbey, Co Down

The house door is outside the main shopfront here. The windows are arcaded and marked by pilasters with projecting corbels supporting the entablature.

Downpatrick, Co Down   **Strabane, Co Tyrone**   **Ballycastle, Co Antrim**

When shop windows began to be more significant some were projected out as bow windows. Gray's printing press with its shallow small-paned window dates from the 18th century, and the Downpatrick shop is probably early 19th century. The grander shop in Ballycastle is probably late 19th century.

Portglenone, Co Antrim

An unusual shop window, looking like a tripartite one but actually made up of two sashes.

Ardglass, Co Down

With a display of Halloween masks, footballs and Fairy liquid, this shop has a divided tripartite window.

Ardglass, Co Down

At this hotel the window may have had horizontal divisions at one time, but they have been removed.

Antrim, Co Antrim

A late 19th century printer's shop, with some recent work on display. Taxi numbers, as evidenced by the shop on the left, used to be more memorable.

Ballycastle, Co Antrim

If you really want your shop to catch the eye, it is hard to beat a couple of Ionic columns, particularly the one between the door and the bow window of the shop.

269

Saintfield, Co Down

This shopfront from about 1885 has a single iron column with a lotus-flower capital supporting the lintel across the wide shop opening.

Ballycastle, Co Antrim

Between the window and the entablature a ventilation strip in the form of patterned perforations was often inserted. This shop has particularly elaborate framing to the windows.

Warrenpoint, Co Down

This particularly handsome shopfront has massive Doric columns on either side of the house door.

Newry, Co Down; Lagan Street, Belfast; Cookstown, Co Tyrone

At either end of the shop entablature, and sometimes more often, elaborately carved corbels were often placed, usually with scrolled volutes and organic decoration. The Newry example has a pedimented top, the Cookstown one a Corinthian base.

(clockwise from bottom left) **Victoria Street, Belfast; Albertbridge Road, Belfast; Saintfield, Co Down; Armagh, Co Armagh; Enniskillen, Co Fermanagh**

On the left, a couple of corbels dangling their legs over the entablature, and a big and little brother; then three different treatments of scrolls in corbels, the centre one with flourishing acanthus leaves.

Ballycastle, Co Antrim; Ballycastle, Co Antrim; Victoria Street, Belfast; Portrush, Co Antrim

The example on the left is particularly flat (with a mask-like face on it), and the one next to it particularly deep. The Victoria Street example pairs corbels and adds an ellipse between them, while the Portrush example is in a style characteristic of the 1920s with its dropped pendants.

Bessbrook, Co Armagh; Carnlough, Co Antrim; Saintfield, Co Down

Probably the first tradesmen to erect an internationally recognised trade sign were the barber surgeons. Their red and white striped pole referred to the blood they produced not when shaving you but when removing a tooth or a leg as they were nothing if not versatile. Some Georgian customers had more to complain about than bad hair days.

Antrim, Co Antrim; Donegall Street, Belfast; Derry, Co L'derry

The glass poles with spinning stripes appear to date mostly from between the wars; the painted lamp-post is an unmissable new take on the theme. Sadly modern hairdressers seem to be abandoning poles for puns as the sign of their trade, though the example in Derry certainly occupies a handsome building.

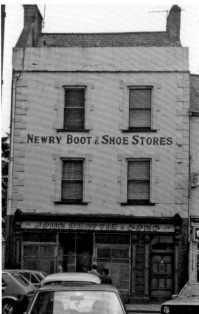

Ballycastle, Co Antrim; Tandragee, Co Armagh; Newry, Co Down

Crowds admiring the latest in footwear at Barton's in Ballycastle; a handsome display of shoes in Tandragee (with an old enamel sign for Holdfast Boots placed just above the Give Way sign); and the magnificent boot emporium in Newry, whose corbels can be seen more closely on p.270. Sadly, shoemakers have now become mere shoe shops.

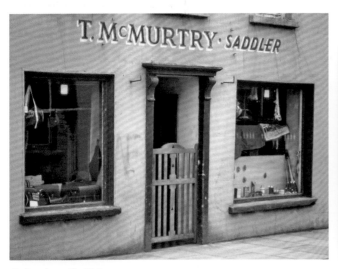

Coleraine, Co L'derry

Few towns now boast a saddler. Although the windows here are modernised, the corbelled doorway and its wooden gate hark back to earlier times.

Bessbrook, Co Armagh

An attractive urban vernacular house with unusual central chimney stacks, which has been adapted for use by a tailor and draper who has enlarged the left hand window.

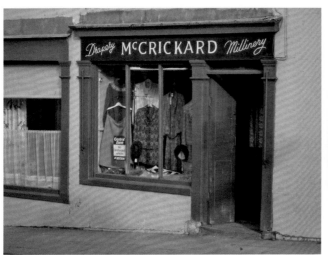

Ballynahinch, Co Down

A draper and milliner selling the latest in very conservative coats and a couple of hats suitable for wearing in church. There is no sophistication in the hand-painted lettering of the sign either.

Cushendall, Co Antrim

Sometimes it is hard to get into Hugh McAteer's shop for the quantity of coats and boots hanging on display in the entrance. The door on the right is to the house.

274

Dromara, Co Down

A charming window display of everything needed for going back to school, including the parked lollipop sign.

Kilkeel, Co Down

Part of a wide draper's display, including the varnished shop door with its cursive gold-leaf lettering.

Warrenpoint, Co Down

A shopfront with rather stylish 1930s lettering and a wooden gate. Obviously where you'd have got white tie and tails.

Kilkeel, Co Down

In a fishing port a draper has to offer not just balls of wool for the women but also seamen's outfits to replace those lost or shrunk at sea.

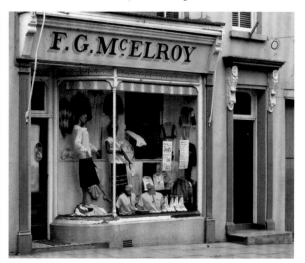

Gilford, Co Down

A very elegant drapery shop complete with blinds and curved shop window. The same paint scheme is carried over to the house door on the right.

Dromara, Co Down

A simple grocer's shop with an unassuming display of cleansing agents, soap powders, pickles and HP sauce.

Comber, Co Down

Probably the most spectacular grocer's shop in Northern Ireland, Macdonald's front is based on red and black granite with gilded lettering and some sophisticated Art Nouveau panels over the windows.

Cushendall, Co Antrim

A neatly painted shopfront with plasterwork fluted pilasters, three-dimensional lettering, and a blind to keep the sunshine off the fine meats within.

Cookstown, Co Tyrone

A quirky façade with heads of animals over every window and bulls' heads emerging from the foliage in the side capitals.

(clockwise) **Larne, Co Antrim; Ballynahinch, Co Down; Warrenpoint, Co Down**

Butchers' shops often used glazed tiles for cleanliness, which opened up the possibility of getting tiles painted with heads of cows and sheep. Note also the very open cast-iron ventilation strips over window and door, and the mosaic entrance. The Ballynahinch shop was designed by Hobart & Heron in 1914; McElroy's metal porch suggests they displayed meat outside.

Gilford, Co Down

Markethill, Co Armagh

Chemists' shops are often quite grand and old-fashioned, the commercial equivalent of a long-established solicitor's practice, and details of such shops appear elsewhere in the book. These two examples are at the cutting edge of post-war pharmacies, advertising Ilford and Kodak rather than those mysterious flasks of coloured water.

Coalisland, Co Tyrone

Warrenpoint, Co Down

This imposing frontage of dark green tiles and gold-leaf lettering represents a combined business of grocery and pharmacy - grocers often combined their trade with other trades like hardware.

An ice cream parlour painted in vanilla and pistachio in a manner certain to attract thirsty customers on a hot day.

Glenarm, Co Antrim

A spacious café with pilasters and arcaded windows. It has since acquired Tourist Board approval and random stone facings but lost some of its charm.

York Street, Belfast

The wartime spirit apparent at this café which retains some of its freestanding lettering in the midst of roadworks and redevelopment.

Portrush, Co Antrim

Nearly hiddden behind the new flat name board is a splendid Edwardian shopfront with slender columns and curved glass.

Derry, Co L'derry

Magnificent lettering and a startlingly cheerful colour scheme draw the eye to this façade more effectively than any plastic signs or unnecessary awnings.

Portrush, Co Antrim

The former Trocadero Café - its Art Nouveau door and small-paned window and the entrance mosaic still surviving.

Moneymore, Co L'derry

The main post office of a town was where one would have gone (as the enamel signs remind us) for postal telegraphs and money orders, and where today fishing licences may be purchased.

Glenarm, Co Antrim

The double-fronted post office with its wide fanlight and two-leaf door has a house door on the right all integrated under the same entablature. The postbox had to be integrated into the small panes of the windows.

Greyabbey, Co Down

Another Money Order Office and Savings Bank, with the letterbox squeezed in alongside other displays.

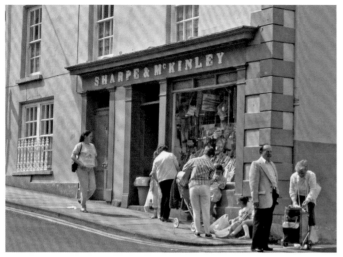

Ballycastle, Co Antrim

Ballycastle, Co Antrim

Undoubtedly the town with the best collection of shopfronts in Ulster is Ballycastle. Sharpe & McKinley's hardware shop is particularly splendid, and even the wool shop looks prosperous. The Auld Lammas Fair takes place in the town at the end of August each year, and its continuing success derives in part from the traditional shops.

Ballycastle, Co Antrim

Ballycastle, Co Antrim

With a fairly simple shopfront, the newsagent makes a brave display of greetings cards and children's annuals. Even the empty shops are kept freshly painted, as many of the buildings still have families living "over the shop" and after all these are their front doors.

281

Comber, Co Down

Early pubs were either inns or simply rooms in a house. This pub still has a strongly domestic character, with the pub only advertised by a couple of windows, the door and a discreet sign.

Rostrevor, Co Down

Later, windows were enlarged but etched glass was then required to regain privacy and reduce the brightness.

Ballycastle, Co Antrim

The advertisement for Old Bushmills whiskey provides the necessary screening for this pub with its arcaded windows and panelled door reveals.

Enniskillen, Co Fermanagh

A house and pub combination, the house door being panelled and the pub one a two-leaf type. The lettering is painted on to the entablature with gold leaf.

Donaghadee, Co Down   **Ballygawley, Co Tyrone**

A common way of marking the pub was to put the owner's name (or later a more fanciful one) in a plaster surround, with lettering in relief, usually replete with full stops. Sometimes the plasterwork would extend to moulded surrounds for the windows and doors as well.

Ballygawley, Co Tyrone

An interesting combination of whimsical shell decoration with avant-garde chrome lettering.

Derry, Co L'derry

Well-incised and serifed lettering over a bar dating from around 1900, with rounded corners to the upper lights of its windows and broad Corinthian pilasters supporting heavy corbels.

Great Victoria Street, Belfast

The most famous pub in Belfast (a great many interesting ones didn't survive the bombing campaigns of the 1970s) is the Crown Bar, with its richly tiled façade and interior packed with snugs.

Derry, Co L'derry

The pepperpot oriel window and Art Nouveau decoration on this pub dates from the end of the 19th century.

Ballycastle, Co Antrim

Plaster enrichments here create panelled pilasters, the comfortably rounded window cill, entablature and much of the lettering.

Portrush, Co Antrim

Swashbuckling lettering, panelled pilasters and glass curved in towards the entrance give promise of a comfortable interior. The combination of dark green with red highlights works well.

Antrim, Co Antrim

At one time garages served petrol through hoses attached to overhead gantries, often overseen by the Michelin man.

Enniskillen, Co Fermanagh

If you sell cars or motorbikes it is hard to keep them in your small showroom and they sometimes spill onto the street, so you may as well add some advertisements as well to tell people what you sell.

Cushendall, Co Antrim

It is surprising how often children arrive at the seaside without their bucket and spade, windmill and football.

Derrygonnelly, Co Fermanagh

Few towns now have a proper hardware shop like this one displaying the full range of spades, forks, rakes and calor gas canisters required by the average farmer. Even this one obviously had to supplement its income with supermarket goods.

Loughgall, Co Armagh

This shop ceased trading in 1950, but even then its system of cupboards and hooks was becoming antiquated.

Church Lane, Belfast

Miss Moran's tobacconists still survives with its enticing (even to a non-smoker) display of cigars and baccy.

Holywood, Co Down

The end of a long wet day at Ted's fruit shop, with most of the veg already sold and the rain pouring down.

Newtownards, Co Down

The customer seems to be considering the policewomen's caps as well as the more conventional millinery on display.

Albertbridge Road, Belfast

The three golden balls advertising the pawnbroker are perhaps the oldest trade sign still found today.

Donegal Quay, Belfast

The famous ship chandlers beside the old steamer docks, with its lifebelt and block and tackle inviting trade.

Ann Street, Belfast

Johnston's golden umbrella moved to Anne Street from an earlier location in Donegall Place.

Castlerock, Co L'derry; East Bridge Street, Belfast; Donaghadee, Co Down; Kilrea, Co L'derry

The chemist in Castlerock refers to the Greek physician Hippocrates, while the 1905 Electric Lighting Station features a hand clutching lightning bolts on its keystone. Occasionally modern businesses devise imaginative trade signs like the vet in Donaghadee and (perhaps less attractively) the plumber in Kilrea.

Lettering

Most architecture, however functional, is abstract. Even lettering looked at closely is abstract, but rather like music it can suggest meanings or emotions that reinforce, or sometimes even contradict, the literal meaning of the words it spells.

Lettering on memorials is designed to last for generations, and can be beautifully incised. More often texts are painted on walls or windows to direct visitors or attract attention, and as they become redundant they are replaced or fade into obscurity. Occasionally two layers of lettering can be found on top of one another and sometimes both have become redundant.

Shop signs identify trades and names, and the type and quality of the lettering say much about the business. There is a plethora of information to be read around our streets - milestones, plaques recording donations, licences, street names, religious texts and irreligious mottoes. But the way that information is spelled out can make even mundane facts a delight to read.

Union Street, Belfast

Lettering comes in all shapes and sizes and many degrees of sophistication, but sometimes the content rises above the quality of the calligraphy. This mysterious message reads "No Topless Bathing", and, partly obscured below it, "Ulster has suffered enough".

Donaghadee, Co Down

Donaghadee, Co Down

All graveyards dating to the 18th century and earlier have many examples of beautifully carved Roman lettering, often on slate which takes a clean and durable mark. Usually the mason was more concerned about the appearance of his lettering than about spelling mistakes or the omission of occasional letters.

Dungannon, Co Tyrone

Even when filled with moss and almost illegible, old stone carving can be beautiful, albeit in a melancholy way befitting graveyards.

Ballyculter, Co Down

Although there is probably a simple explanation like death from an infectious disease, it is tempting to speculate whether the firm instruction above arises from the activities of vampires.

Toomebridge, Co Antrim

John Cary again, unsure whether he was going up or down after death (though there is a hand on top pointing up).

Killough, Co Down

The grave of the engineer and inventor Rex McCandless, with a sort of dymo label riveted onto the slate.

Castledawson, Co L'derry

Gravestones get covered in ivy, memorial seats get sat upon, but the clock face on the church tower is read every day.

Ballygowan, Co Down

A reminder on the workhouse tower that the end is nigh, when you only wondered if there was honey still for tea.

Castleward, Co Down

Seaforde, Co Down

Another way to ensure your immortality was to endow almshouses - Sophie Ward's was to house "four decayed females" and the Seaforde ones were "erected and endowed at the request of the late Mrs Forde" in 1828.

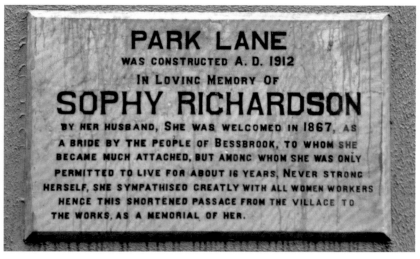

Glenarm, Co Antrim;
Comber, Co Down

Two date stones with a carefree approach to grammar and spelling.

Bessbrook, Co Armagh

Plaque on a "shortened passage" in the mill village of Bessbrook, recording the rather touching reason for its creation and inviting the thanks of the mill's women workers.

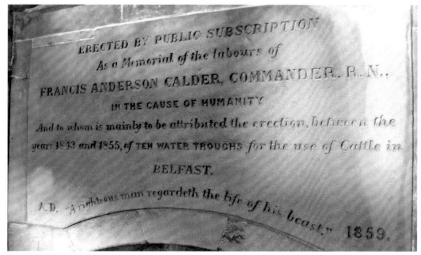

Calder Fountain, Belfast

Lieutenant Calder was the founder of the Ulster Society for the Prevention of Cruelty to Animals, and erected water troughs for horses and cattle. This structure has fountains for human use on the sides as well as troughs for animals.

Rostrevor, Co Down;
Ballyeaston, Co Antrim

Memorial heating apparatus and a National Schools plaque of 1840.

Gracehill, Co Antrim

Comber, Co Down

Ballymena, Co Antrim

A proud builder or client will often put the date on his completed building, usually in stone. This is fine, but can be misleading when the building is demolished and a historically-minded rebuilder incorporates it in his new building, giving it an erroneous antiquity. The Ballymena lettering is particularly free for its date, as if made of coiled rope.

Newry, Co Down

Royal Avenue, Belfast

If the date is built into the brickwork (*left*) or part of the stucco plasterwork up at roof level (*right*) you can be pretty sure that it is correct. On later Victorian buildings there was often quite a game in finding places to put the date or monograms where they could be seen but wouldn't be immediately obvious.

Greyabbey, Co Down

Crumlin Road, Belfast

Lurgan, Co Armagh

Just as the death of Prince Albert spawned a lot of memorial towers, Queen Victoria's jubilee inspired many projects in 1887. The VR monogram and crown can be found on a number of buildings, here (*centre*) inside Crumlin Road gaol. The practice of putting dates or monograms at the base of chimney stacks was also common in the late 19th century.

Hampton Park, Belfast

By the end of the 19th century free forms of lettering had evolved that made it quite difficult to read some dates.

Antrim, Co Antrim

You would have thought that anyone asked to carve the date on the local courthouse would have taken the time to sketch it out first and check the spelling. But perhaps this was only a bit of graffiti carved on as an afterthought.

Dungiven, Co L'derry; Donaghadee, Co Down; Ormeau Road, Belfast; Newry, Co Down

Sometimes hand-painted street signs are still to be found, or appropriate signs like the tarryblack paint on whitewash for the harbour office in Donaghadee (*lower left*). Belfast streets were all labelled in black and white tiles (*centre*) but most have been altered over the years. Milestones are always unique to their location.

Newtownards, Co Down; Randalstown, Co Antrim; Hillsborough, Co Down; Armagh, Co Armagh

Milestones were generally made of iron but could take a variety of forms either freestanding (*left and second from left*) or set into a wall or post (*second from right*). The enamel advertisement (*right*) which appears standardised is in fact also a milestone (saying it is half a mile to Armagh).

Lurgan, Co Armagh

Fine lettering sliding down the gable parallel to the roof slope, in the shadow of an impressive set of chimney pots. Gable signs were popular in Victorian times, when people were more accustomed to looking up.

Randalstown, Co Antrim

When surfaces are repainted the quality of old signs can be lost, and it is often preferable to see the faint original.

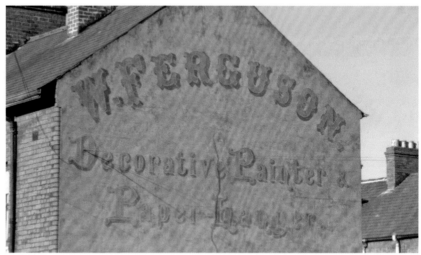

Donegall Road, Belfast

"Pam-Roy Pastry Pleases People" can be seen faintly on the gable in the shadow of the City Hospital.

Mowhan Street, Belfast

A decorative painter showing off his lettering in a gable advertisement probably of about 1920. Painters often hung wallpaper as well as it required skill to trim the paper which came with blank edges.

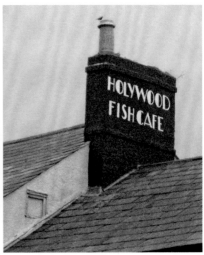

York Street, Belfast

Rather brashly, whole painted façades of Victorian buildings could become giant poster hoardings.

Derry, Co L'derry

The rather sombre premises of the Madden Mineral Water Co, with the lettering integral to the design.

Holywood, Co Down

A comparatively modern painted sign on a chimney, looking like a single-funnelled ship.

Warrenpoint, Co Down

The chemist advertises on his roof, the Malocca family advertise their teas and ices on the gable of their café. Gables present a challenge to sign painters fitting words in.

Arthur Square, Belfast

Sometimes when a shopfront is stripped a much older one is revealed, such as this one advertising Tyler's Boots for Style and Wear. Unfortunately they are usually quickly hidden again.

Carnlough, Co Antrim

The magnificent Edwardian stucco frontage of McAuley's Hotel: due to European regulations defining what constitutes a hotel, the word has had to be painted out since.

The Mount, Belfast

The shape of this building does a lot of the advertising work, but the large freestanding lettering is undoubtedly eye-catching.

Lurgan, Co Armagh

Sometimes the simplest forms of lettering are most effective. The sign picks up the colour of the quoins and puts the name at the top like the title of a book.

Newry, Co Down

Magnificent lettering with a golden outline and double shadow in pink and black over corbels with luscious fruits - and all this is on a shoe store (*see* p.273).

(*from top*) **Augher, Co Tyrone; Downpatrick, Co Down; Ballynahinch, Co Down; Coleraine, Co L'derry; Antrim, Co Antrim; Maghera, Co L'derry**

A selection of hand-painted shop signs, for a grocer, a chemist, a tobacconist, a laundry and two pubs respectively. Sans serif is generally despised.

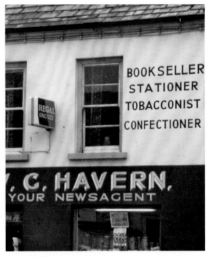

Warrenpoint, Co Down

Newsagents have to be Jacks-of-all-trades, but few would now sell stationery and books.

Cornmarket, Belfast

The Art Deco trademark on the Woolworth-Burton building of 1930. The ornament is rather Egyptian.

(clockwise from top left) **Donegall Street, Belfast; Dungannon, Co Tyrone; Kilkeel, Co Down; Lurgan, Co Armagh; Donegall Place, Belfast; Cookstown, Co Tyrone; Donegall Square, Belfast; Ballycastle, Co Antrim; Cushendall, Co Antrim; Dungannon, Co Tyrone**

Examples of shadowed lettering, three-dimensional lettering and one chrome sans serif example of about 1950.

(from top) **Lurgan, Co Armagh; Kilkeel, Co Down; Killyleagh, Co Down; Ballygawley, Co Tyrone; Saintfield, Co Down**

From the intricate palimpsest at the top to chrome.

(from top) **Ballyshannon, Co Donegal; Great Victoria Street, Belfast; Lisburn Road, Belfast; Bedford Street, Belfast**

Lettering on glass - gold leaf behind glass and composition lettering in front of glass.

Warrenpoint, Co Down

An extraordinary very long shop fascia of cast iron with the lettering cast into it and the Greek key pattern with guttae (coloured red) over it.

Comber, Co Down

A detail of the wonderful Macdonald's shop (*see* p.276) with its incised gold leaf lettering cut into granite and the sombre green tiles set off by bright red highlights.

Ballynahinch, Co Down

The Primrose Bar's golden lettering involves a layer of black paint behind glass leaving gaps behind which gold leaf can be applied. There is also delicately patterned etched glass in the window.

Woodstock Road, Belfast; Warrenpoint, Co Down

Gold leaf behind glass was commonly used for house or terrace names.

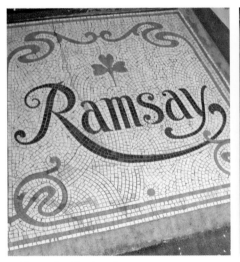

Ballycastle, Co Antrim

Many shops put their names in mosaic at their front door like a welcome mat, and a few have survived long after the shops.

Moy, Co Tyrone

A stained glass privacy screen to a pub. The white glass is legible outside while the colours can be appreciated inside.

Helen's Bay, Co Down

The Dufferin monogram incorporated in the Marquis' personal railway station.

Royal Avenue, Belfast

A bronze plaque at the entrance to the offices of Northern Ireland's main evening paper.

Newry, Co Down; Bangor, Co Down

Contrasting nameplates for a Victorian warehouse (*top*) and a 1930s block of flats (*below*).

Sussex Place, Belfast

Carved stone plaque over the entrance to convent schools of 1878, with a flourishing bunch of shamrocks.

Donegall Square North, Belfast

This was originally the entrance to a linen warehouse of 1864, hence the swags of linen over the door, which remain entirely appropriate fot the present occupants, the Linen Hall Library.

Kilkeel, Co Down

For a few years around 1890 the Cyclists' Touring Club issued signs with a "Repairers to" category like this.

Kilkeel and Rostrevor, Co Down

Pub licences recorded in gold leaf over the front door. Sometimes they add "But not to sell on Sunday".

Derry, Co L'derry

Graffiti on the hoarding round the site of the threatened Tillie & Henderson shirt factory in 2002, apparently questioning the legitimacy of the actions of developers, arsonists, planners and conservationists alike.

(*clockwise from top left*) **Ballynahinch, Co Down; Aughnacloy, Co Tyrone; Coleraine, Co L'derry; Randalstown, Co Antrim; Brookeborough, Co Fermanagh**

Enamel signs were mass produced and distributed like modern posters, but stayed around for more years. The Fry's Chocolate image was used on the chocolate and was very familiar ("Desperation, Pacification, Expectation, Acclamation, Realization").

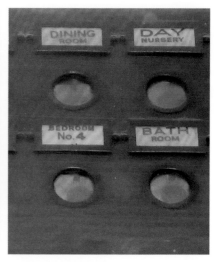

Florencecourt, Co Fermanagh

The library of this thatched cottage, mainly Bumper Adventure Books, was kept under the steep stairs.

Blackhead, Co Antrim

Lighthouse keepers were supplied with reading matter stored in these cupboards and regularly changed.

Bangor, Co Down

Part of the servants' bells in a middle class house of 1936. After the war, however, the number of servants declined.

Ballydugan, Co Down

There is a tradition of plasterers and painters leaving their names and dates on their work, and of their successors respecting them and adding their own. These names are pencilled on the inside of a rural shutter.

Ballydugan, Co Down

A few contemporary builders still take the time to leave their signatures. This one often leaves a print of his hand.

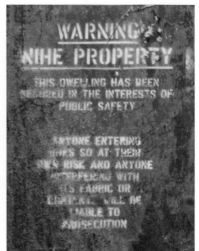

Ballynahinch, Co Down

However clearly painted or printed, some signs are still hard to follow. Fewer words, and a bit of politeness, are generally more effective. And since the sign is going to be up for a while, taking a bit of trouble with the lettering is appreciated.

Enniskillen, Co Fermanagh

Lawnbrook Avenue, Belfast

Official signs in stencilled lettering are ominous, and in this case almost certainly spells the end of the house.

Ballintoy, Co Antrim

No doubt about the boundaries of Bendhu, the eccentric house built at Ballintoy by the artist Newton Penprase - the steps at the bottom of the stairs cut into the cliff say "Strictly Private", and then in case you didn't believe it, "Yes".

Kilwaughter, Co Antrim

It's always well to be prepared for what you are going to find at the end of the lane.

307

Decoration

Nearly everything in this book has had something to do with decoration, and it might be felt that there is no need for another chapter on the subject. But while a door or a window may be decorative, it does primarily serve a function. When you put a head on a keystone, or hide an animal in the shrubbery of your capital, you are going beyond function into the realms of the imagination.

Many of the heads found on buildings belong to mythological or generic figures, but they are carefully chosen to add gravitas or beauty. Animals are more often added to provide an element of fantasy and fun, while abstract decoration may be used to place a building in a particular fashionable style, or link it symbolically to its purpose.

Modern architects have lost the desire to decorate their buildings, and too often their clients feel that decoration is beneath their dignity or merely an unnecessary expense. Looking at the richness of so many Victorian buildings one is bound to feel nostalgia for an age that was able to provide such fun in its architecture and pose so many riddles and references to ages past and present as well as enclosing space.

Donegall Street, Belfast

William Hastings designed this building in the 1870s for the *Belfast News Letter*. As befits the premises of what is now the oldest daily newspaper still being published (it first appeared in 1737), the eight heads on its façade include early publishers and Mercury, the winged messenger of the gods.

(clockwise from top left) **Cookstown, Co Tyrone; Caledon, Co Armagh; Dungannon, Co Tyrone; Bangor, Co Down; Derry, Co L'derry; Newtownards Road, Belfast**

The 17th century door lintel in Cookstown carries the Lindsay family crest; the Caledon arms are supported by a mermaid and an elephant; the lion and unicorn are alert at Derry but almost comatose in Dungannon.

310

Ballywalter, Co Down

The animals in coats of arms are often large, unlike this little hermaphrodite winged mock-gargoyle.

Hampton Park, Belfast

Cast-iron spandrels are usually of scrolls and flowers; these ones enjoy the thrill of entwined dragons.

Virginia Street, Belfast

Similar at first sight, Belfast terrace houses are full of surprises, like this monkey's head between front doors.

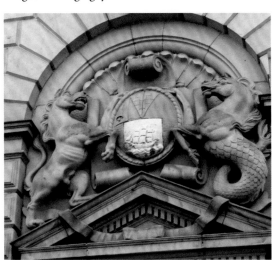

Armagh, Co Armagh

The chained wolf and seahorse support a Belfast coat of arms, for the Belfast Banking Co (just as the Ulster Bank, *facing page*, uses the red hand of Ulster).

Ormeau Road, Belfast

The gable of the Klondyke Building at the gasworks carries a gigantic coat of arms - the scale can be judged by the two people at the base. The Belfast arms on the facing page was at the ropeworks.

Moy, Co Tyrone

A particularly long-tongued lion with one clawed foot over an early 19th century entrance.

Warrenpoint, Co Down

A lion relaxing on top of a crowstep gable being monarch of all he surveys. Behind him, a good stack of chimney pots.

Lurgan, Co Armagh

A lion in his own niche guarding the entrance door to a house. Mass wall construction enables such niches.

Lisburn, Co Antrim

A particularly handsome lion patrolling over a shopfront. He probably dates from the middle of the 19th century, when carved lions and eagles were not uncommon guardians of shops and pubs.

Castle Lane, Belfast

A highly stylised lion from the 1920s, hiding under an equally stylised Ionic capital and with a mouthful of fasces.

Donegall Square West, Belfast

A detail from the roofline of a large late Victorian Classical building. Sculptures in copper depicting a dolphin and a sphinx contrast with the Renaissance stonework.

Mount Stewart, Co Down

The gardens at Mount Stewart are full of concrete dinosaurs, dodos and other animals, satirising the politicians that used to visit.

Ballintoy, Co Antrim

The stark Mondriancsque concrete house near the harbour is enlivened by mythological beasts over the No Parking sign.

Banbridge, Co Down

The memorial to Capt Crozier, second in command on HMS Terror, the ship in which Capt Franklin sought the North West Passage, has four polar bears at its base.

Richhill, Co Armagh (*top left*); **Carlisle Circus, Belfast** (*the rest*)

A surprising feature amongst the tall chimneys of the 17th century house at Richhill is an eagle ready to take off. Victorian buildings often carry grotesque or humorous depictions of animals in the mediaeval manner, but one particularly rich in such ornament was St Enoch's Church at Carlisle Circus.

University Square, Belfast

A gargoyle which used to spit rainwater clear of the building, now superseded by a new hopper and downpipe.

Enniskillen, Co Fermanagh

Looking rather like a gargoyle, this gryphon is a stop end on a stone string course.

Cookstown, Co Tyrone

An unusually blue and belligerent-looking gryphon surmounting a gate pillar.

Mount Stewart, Co Down

One of the more conventional animals in the Mount Stewart gardens (*see* p.313) - a gryphon is a winged lion.

Alfred Street, Belfast

The motto is Pure Flax, but the animals appear to be gryphons with the heads of parrots.

Charlemont, Co Armagh

The Eagle Bar is marked with an eagle that has just caught a fish and is not going to share it.

Ballynahinch, Co Down

This bull's head in the spandrel on the front of the shop indicated the presence of a butcher.

Cookstown, Co Tyrone

Probably every bull wants a bigger set of horns, and this one must take some pride in the Ionic volutes behind him.

Portglenone, Co Antrim

A well-observed portrait of a sheep in tiles on the walls of a meat purveyor's premises.

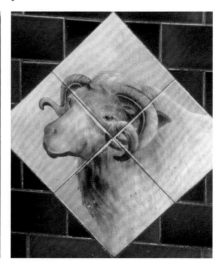

Ballynahinch, Co Down

Warrenpoint, Co Down

Kilkeel, Co Down

Tiles made a hygienic surface to line the walls of butchers' shops, and the common colour scheme was green and white, broken up by pictures of animals depicting what is on sale. Of bulls and sheep at least - for some reason I have never encountered pictures of pigs or chickens in a butcher's shop.

Botanic Avenue, Belfast

A wonderful image of a swan in a top hat, swimming in a sea of pargetting - *see also* p.324.

North Street, Belfast

The Elephant Buildings, with its tile portraits of rather mastodon-like elephants, was erected in 1893, but the elephant over the entrance was transplanted from an earlier building when the street was widened. Just over a hundred years later the elephant mysteriously disappeared, and the building itself has been demolished.

317

High Street, Belfast

An Edwardian building with finely-carved swags of fruit and flowers in sandstone.

Royal Avenue, Belfast

Two of a series of decorated pilasters on a building of 1883: others include a parrot in a fruit tree, an owl under the moon, a heron, a lyre-bird, and a monkey hanging on by its tail.

University Square, Belfast

With the formal orders often ignored by the end of the 19th century, even a small capital could be elaborate.

Donegall Road, Belfast

The grapes at the entrance to a church suggest the communion wine might be of good quality.

Armagh, Co Armagh

The sculptor of this capital had a bit of fun by adding a monster after carving the corn on the cob.

Victoria Street, Belfast

The Lytle's and McCausland's seed warehouses of 1868 are so covered with sculpture (*see left and elsewhere*) that few people notice the sprouting peas just under the cornice, typical of sculptor Thomas Fitzpatrick's wit and imagination.

Victoria Street, Belfast

Two capitals from the McCausland building, a parrot over cornflowers (*top*) and blackbirds in cosy nests (*below*).

Old Holywood Road, Belfast

By 1862, when these were made, a sculptor could be given free rein in the carving of a capital, and while the outline of an Ionic or Corinthian capital can be descried in the shrubbery, it is less important than the virtuosic depiction of leaves and petals.

(clockwise from top left) **Glenarm, Co Antrim; Newry, Co Down; Waring Street, Belfast (twice); Lurgan, Co Armagh; Victoria Street, Belfast; Castle Place, Belfast; Derry, Co L'derry; Crumlin, Co Antrim**

A collection of male heads - a Bacchus, a satyr and several river gods (probably); then, representing Ulster's trade routes, a Chinaman, an Oriental (or possibly Elizabethan) gentleman, a Turk and two Pharaohs on the house of an army general.

(clockwise from top left) **Donegall Square South, Belfast; Queen Street, Belfast; Rugby Road, Belfast; Haypark Avenue, Belfast; Lurgan, Co Armagh; Donegall Place, Belfast**

On Jaffé's linen warehouse on Donegall Square South are heads of Shakespeare, Michelangelo, Homer and Jacquard who invented the damask loom; Sir Arthur Chichester is in Queen Street; and Australia is still being unveiled on Donegall Place.

(clockwise from top left) **Lurgan, Co Armagh; Jennymount Mill, Belfast; Ormeau Avenue, Belfast; Victoria Street, Belfast**

Shakespeare was a popular figure to add class to a building, particularly if it was industrial. The Thompson Fountain in Ormeau Avenue has heads of mediaeval kings and queens - one (under restoration) with a monocle and Dundreary whiskers. But the most celebrated heads are the continents and their fruits on the former McCausland seed warehouse.

322

Donegall Square West, Belfast

These cherubs are having a tug o'war with Belfast rope (the ropeworks were the biggest in the world).

Royal Avenue, Belfast

This head looks idealised and produced for a keystone that could have been placed in any building.

Rostrevor, Co Down

A pensive lady forming a stop end for the eyebrow over a doorway. The tilt of her head makes it look like a portrait.

Bangor, Co Down

A Dutch gable on a building at the seafront is ornamented by two youngsters that look about to get down for a paddle.

Shaftesbury Square, Belfast

The sculptures by Elizabeth Frink on the side of a bank have become known as Draft and Overdraft.

Waring Street, Belfast

Being Victorian sculptures and obviously depicting Britannia, Justice and Commerce, these need no nicknames.

Donegall Square East, Belfast

The Titanic Memorial beside the City Hall marks the tragedy in a wistful group of sea nymphs and a drowned sailor.

Derry, Co L'derry

The vogue for casting them in metal always makes the scales of Justice look rather precarious.

Derry, Co L'derry

An almost Italianate group of figures above an ornamented pediment look down over the city.

Stranmillis Road, Belfast

One of the fine Victorian tombstones in Friar's Bush Cemetery, this depicts an Irish harp in a wreath of shamrocks.

Botanic Avenue, Belfast

The inventor of this fake half-timbered building was said to have made his fortune designing film sets for Errol Flynn films and wanted to leave a similar mark on his native city. Every panel was differently ornamented (*see* p.317).

Whitehead, Co Antrim

This otherwise unremarkable house is decorated with an anchor on the front wall.

Derry, Co L'derry

An anchor in plaster decorates the City of Derry Boating Club's tower. There is a racing pennant on the other side.

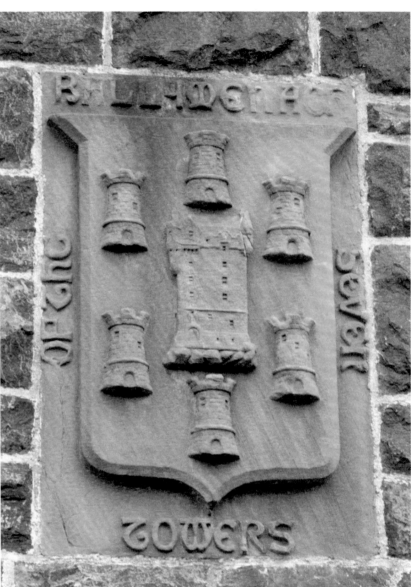

Ballymena, Co Antrim

The gate lodge to the People's Park is decorated with a series of red sandstone plaques. This one refers to Ballymena's Seven Towers, the largest of which was Ballymena Castle (in the centre), demolished in the 1950s.

Newtownbutler, Co Fermanagh

Galloon graveyard has a number of these early *memento mori* gravestones with a skull and crossbones.

Boa Island, Co Fermanagh

The famous Janus stone with its two heads front and back may date from the Iron Age.

Derrylin, Co Fermanagh

This figure carved about 1850 is said to represent King Billy, though it looks more like Billy the Kid.

Comber, Co Down

This 18th century gentleman used to grace a back entry but has moved on without leaving a clue to his identity.

College Square East, Belfast

"The Black Man", who is actually green, gets his name from the statue of the Earl of Belfast that formerly stood there.

Donegall Street, Belfast

One of the newest statues to arrive in Belfast, which has gained in recent years from a clear out of Soviet statues.

High Street, Belfast

Inside St George's Church is this memorial to Sir Henry Pottinger, who negotiated the British lease on Hong Kong in 1842.

Royal Avenue, Belfast

It looks as if there is an Oriental connection also to this sculpture on a building of 1881, though a second doorcase with a matching sculpture is lost and with it the story behind it.

Hillsborough, Co Down

Pub signs are not very common in Ulster, though this shifty-looking parson is an excellent example.

Ballymena, Co Antrim

David Herbison, the Bard of Dunclug, was a weaver poet, who wrote in the local vernacular.

Bangor, Co Down

The housework is never done for this figure of Victory, forever waving her palm frond.

The setting

Buildings don't exist in a vacuum. They form part of a streetscape or a landscape, and they may have a garden or their owners may wish they had one and create something anyhow. In cities the hard landscaping of cobble or flag draws on the native geology just as the building itself does.

Whatever way the architect or builder left it when he went off the site, a building changes through time and one of the most obvious ways is how the natural world grows up or is cultivated around it.

Conservatories bring gardens into the house quite literally, and were very popular in the 19th century with even quite modest houses attaching a glasshouse onto the side (if necessary the north side in the case of a semi).

There are those garden sheds that grow into holiday homes in their own right. And finally, there are those gardens that grow beyond topiary into realms of fantasy, leaving architecture far behind...

Ballyalton, Co Down

Topiary demands many years of patience and an eye for the sometimes surprising shapes that lie within bushes. The best examples are often not associated with interesting buildings, but they are a form of architecture in their own right.

Armagh, Co Armagh

"Armagh marble" flags laid in the back yard of a house. Neatly jointed, and able to take up irregular shapes.

Hill Street, Belfast

Coyle's Place, Belfast

The streets of Belfast were formerly paved with setts but complaints were made about the noise of cartwheels on the irregular surface, and they required skill to lift and relay when services were introduced, so were gradually replaced with tarmac.

Gracehill, Co Antrim

Kerbs were commonly made of granite (*upper right*) or bluestone as here, giving a strong local character to the roads.

Saintfield, Co Down

Rectangular setts may have been used in Belfast, but in towns they tended to be irregular cobbles.

Donaghmore, Co Down

A neatly laid farmyard covered in roughly-squared granite setts. Stonework skills were very strong in south Down.

Holywood, Co Down

Glenarm, Co Antrim

Templepatrick, Co Antrim

Using small cobbles of contrasting limestone and basalt or shale it was possible to achieve a variety of patterns with little difficulty, whether an outline pattern (*left*) or more distinct diamonds (*centre*). A less common pattern was one of black and white stripes (*right*).

Downpatrick, Co Down

In east Down the local rock makes small rounded pebbles that enable comfortable walking.

Downpatrick, Co Down

Sometimes the pavement can be laid out with freer designs like the fleur de lis here.

Rosetta Park, Belfast

Victorian and Edwardian houses often had paths from the gate to the front door laid out in ornamental tiles.

331

Comber, Co Down

On one side of the Square in Comber is a remarkable cobbled pavement with lettering that has become illegible through well-meant but inaccurate repairs. There is certainly a gentleman in a frock coat with a walking stick, and what looks like a leaping gazelle. The story is that Master McGrath the winning greyhound was brought up there and he and his master are the figures.

Craigavad, Co Down

A very handsome and well-maintained conservatory with ogival dome. Although conservatories are usually painted white, this shows that dark colours can be very effective.

Crossgar, Co Down

A long range of glasshouses with a tall central section, associated with a walled garden. Big houses used to be almost self-sufficient for fruit and vegetables.

Old Holywood Road, Belfast

This conservatory, very impressive even in dereliction, was probably designed by Thomas Jackson, who lived at the house to which it was attached and which was later occupied by the Ewart linen family. The ironwork includes barley-sugar columns, ogee gutters and spiky crestings, and the dome was nearly as tall as the main house.

Crossgar, Co Down

Sophisticated conservatories would have ranks of iron plant stands (*right*) to display the flowers, and iron grilles let into the floor to let heat rise from the pipes. Many had cranked handles to open inaccessible windows.

Rosetta Park, Belfast

Even quite modest houses would have lean-to conservatories, usually built of wood, to bring on plants for the house.

*All at **Groomsport, Co Down** apart from bottom right at **Ballagh, Co Fermanagh***

Between the wars some families were able to acquire a holiday chalet somewhere beside the sea like Groomsport. These were light wooden buildings on which much time and attention to ornament was lavished. Sadly, most have now been replaced by touring caravans. The cottage at Ballagh is a *cottage orné* on a larger scale.

Moy, Co Tyrone

At one time few houses had an inside toilet, but now outside ones are rare. Particularly rare temples of convenience are three-seaters like this one.

Bangor, Co Down

Too small even for a chalet, this little house has been home for rabbits in the park for over fifty years. It is not known if they appreciate its quirky form.

Donegall Place, Belfast

The Castle Restaurant opened in 1880, named after Belfast Castle, hence the building in the apex.

Castlederg, Co Tyrone

Sometimes beside a modern bungalow will be seen a nostalgic evocation of older cottages.

Gransha, Co Down

This structure at a field boundary appears to be an animal feeding trough disguised as a very wee cottage.

Newtownbutler, Co Fermanagh

A thatched cottage is nothing without a few rambling roses making their way up the wall and mingling with the thatch. However as the occupants work in the fields they don't generally have a garden other than the vegetable patch.

Tate's Avenue, Belfast

When you live in the town, on the other hand, nostalgia for greenery is perfectly natural and sometimes hard to control.

Rostrevor, Co Down

A dense stubble of ivy looks smart and is easy to keep trimmed, though as the roots can penetrate stonework and clog gutters it is not a very good idea. Virginia creeper and wisteria as used on most big houses do less damage.

Derry, Co L'derry

Even ivy can get out of hand, and when you can't see out of the second floor windows it is time to call a gardener.

Portglenone, Co Antrim

The horticultural equivalent of a mask, making it hard to guess what kind of windows lie behind the shrubbery. No doubt it is ideal for nesting birds.

Gracehill, Co Antrim

This looks like a green Loch Ness Monster, although as the neck becomes a pergola rather than a head the likeness may not be deliberate.

Bangor, Co Down; Derrylin, Co Fermanagh

A lively hedge in Bangor, and mysterious geometric shapes near Derrylin.

Clogher, Co Down

Some promising topiary in the making, with what looks like a colony of young rabbits emerging from the hedge. At this stage the gardener has to be very patient as nothing looks very convincing yet.

Ballyalton, Co Down

A well established topiary garden with hens, reindeer, teddy bears and a goat all densely plumaged and on sturdy legs (*see also* p.328).

Kilwarlin, Co Down

Not everyone has room to build a model of the battle of Thermopolae on his front lawn (with a pond representing the Aegean Sea), but the Moravian minister here in the 1830s managed it.

Newcastle, Co Down

Some people like to clutter their mantelpiece with objects, and then move on to their gardens.

Aghinlig, Co Armagh

You start with a few cartwheels and a rocking horse, then add a model house, a wooden barrel, some hubcaps, a couple of birdbaths, some plastic flowers for year-round colour and a plastic stork. But beyond this lies madness...

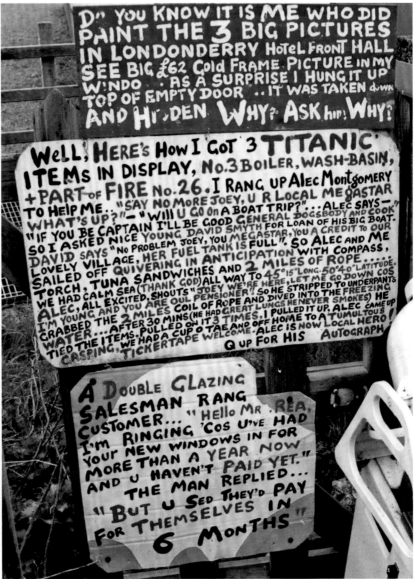

D' YOU KNOW IT IS ME WHO DID PAINT THE 3 BIG PICTURES IN LONDONDERRY HOTEL FRONT HALL SEE BIG £62 Cold FRAME PICTURE IN MY WINDO . AS A SURPRISE I HUNG IT UP TOP OF EMPTY DOOR .. IT WAS TAKEN down AND HIDDEN WHY? ASK him WHY?

WELL, HERE's HOW I GOT 3 TITANIC ITEMS IN DISPLAY, No.3 BOILER, WASH-BASIN, +PART of FIRE No. 26. I RANG UP Alec Montgomery TO HELP ME. "SAY NO MORE JOEY, U R Local ME GASTAR WHAT's UP?" — "WILL U GO On A BOAT TRIP?"...ALEC SAYS — "IF YOU BE CAPTAIN I'LL BE GOOD GENERAL DOGSBODY AND COOK" SO I ASKED NICE YOUNG DAVID SMYTH FOR LOAN OF HIS BIG BOAT. DAVID SAYS "No PROBLEM JOEY, YOU MEGASTAR, YOU A CREDIT TO OUR LOVELY VILLAGE, HER FUEL TANK IS FULL". SO ALEC AND ME SAILED OFF QUIVERING IN ANTICIPATION WITH COMPASS, TORCH, TUNA SANDWICHES AND 2 MILES OF ROPE..... WE HAD CALM SEA (THANK GOD) ALL WAY TO 45°15' LONG. 50°4'0" LATITUDE. ALEC, ALL EXCITED, SHOUTS "JOEY WE'RE HERE, LET ME GO DOWN COS I'M YOUNG AND YOU ARE OUL PENSIONER" SO HE STRIPPED TO UNDERPANTS GRABBED THE 2 MILES COIL OF ROPE AND DIVED INTO THE FREEZING WATER...AFTER 30 MINS (HE HAD GREAT LUNGS HE NEVER SMOKES) HE TIED THE ITEMS, PULLED ON IT 3 TIMES, I PULLED IT UP, ALEC CAME UP GASPING, WE HAD A CUP O TAE AND OFF HOME TO A TUMULTOUS TICKERTAPE WELCOME. ALEC IS NOW Local HERO! Q UP FOR HIS AUTOGRAPH

A DOUBLE GLAZING SALESMAN RANG CUSTOMER... "Hello MR. REA, I'm RINGING 'COS U'VE HAD YOUR NEW WINDOWS IN FOR MORE THAN A YEAR NOW AND U HAVEN'T PAID YET." THE MAN REPLIED... "BUT U SED THEY'D PAY FOR THEMSELVES IN 6 MONTHS"

Carnlough, Co Antrim

For over thirty years (the small photos were taken in 1979 and he had started in 1965) Moscow Joe McKinley, a milkman, decorated his garden, eventually covering it and the house with painted plaques. His attempt "to briten up this drab world" was not appreciated by his wife, who left him in 1991, or his children, who demolished the house when he died in 2003.

INDEX OF PLACES

INDEX OF PLACES

Mack's shoe shop, Ballynahinch, 1979 and 2011

House in tattoo

A young gentleman showing off a bespoke
tattoo showing the house he used to live in,
which is now demolished.

The majority of photographs in this book were taken by the author. However, he is grateful to the late Dick Oram for photographs at pp. 26b, 53e, 55b, 91e, 132f, 135f, 136b, 146b, 150d, 157e, 161b, 218d, 225b, 239c, 242b, 245e, 249b, 274b and 331a, to Peter Haining for the photograph at p.339d, and to Joanna Mules for that at p.57d. The Moscow Joe documentation is from Peter Haining's HIBERNIA project which is now located in the National Visual Art Library at NCAD in Dublin.

Lurgan, Co Armagh